"Mailer continues his familiar shadow-boxing with the ineffable."

—*Time*

"Norman Mailer . . . plunges into the vital spirits of Muhammad Ali and George Foreman . . . and comes up a winner. . . . By fight time the reader has been artfully hoodooed into expecting more from the match than anyone but Mailer saw in it—and amazingly delivers. . . . [He] divides our hearts between Ali and Foreman."

—*Kirkus Reviews*

By Norman Mailer

The Fight

The Fight

Norman Mailer

RANDOM HOUSE TRADE PAPERBACKS

NEW YORK

2013 Random House Trade Paperback Edition

Copyright © 1975 by Norman Mailer

Published in the United States by Random House Trade Paperbacks, an imprint
of The Random House Publishing Group, a division of Random House LLC,
a Penguin Random House Company, New York.

RANDOM HOUSE and the HOUSE colophon
are registered trademarks of Random House LLC.

Originally published in hardcover in the United States
by Little, Brown & Co., Boston, in 1975.

Portions of this book originally appeared in *Playboy* magazine.

Grateful acknowledgment is made to Grove/Atlantic, Inc., and Faber and Faber Ltd. for
permission to reprint an excerpt from *The Palmwine Drunkard* by Amos Tutuola
(published by Faber and Faber Ltd. as *The Palm Wine Drinkard*), copyright © 1953 by
George Braziller, copyright © the Estate of Amos Tutuola. Reprinted by
permission of Grove/Atlantic, Inc., and Faber and Faber Ltd.

Library of Congress Cataloging-in-Publication Data
Mailer, Norman
The fight / Norman Mailer.
p. cm.
Originally published: Boston: Little, Brown, [1975]
ISBN 978-0-8129-8612-9
eBook ISBN 978-0-8129-8596-2
1. Ali, Muhammad, 1942– . 2. Foreman, George, 1949– . 3. Boxing—United States.
I. Title
GV1132.A44M35 1997
796'.83—dc21   97-11107
CIP

Printed in the United States of America on acid-free paper

www.atrandom.com

4   6   8   9   7   5   3

CONTENTS

Part II N'golo

THE DEAD ARE
DYING OF THIRST

1. CARNAL INDIFFERENCE

THERE IS ALWAYS a shock in seeing him again. Not *live* as in television but standing before you, looking his best. Then the World's Greatest Athlete is in danger of being our most beautiful man, and the vocabulary of Camp is doomed to appear. Women draw an *audible* breath. Men look *down*. They are reminded again of their lack of worth. If Ali never opened his mouth to quiver the jellies of public opinion, he would still inspire love and hate. For he is the Prince of Heaven — so says the silence around his body when he is luminous.

When he is depressed, however, his pale skin turns the color of coffee with milky water, no cream. There is the sickly green of a depressed morning in the muddy washes of the flesh. He looks not quite well. That may be a fair description of how he appeared at his training camp in Deer Lake, Pennsylvania, on a September afternoon seven weeks before his fight in Kinshasa with George Foreman.

His sparring was spiritless. Worse. He kept getting hit with stupid punches, shots he would normally avoid, and that was not like Ali! There was an art to watching him train and you acquired it over the years. Other champions picked sparring partners who could imitate the style of their next opponent and, when they could afford it, added a fighter who was congenial: someone they could hit at will, someone fun to box. Ali did this also, but reversed the order. For the second fight with Sonny Liston, his favorite had been Jimmy Ellis, an intricate artist who had nothing in common with Sonny. As boxers, Ellis and Liston had such different moves one could not pass a bowl of soup to the other without spilling it. Of course, Ali had other sparring partners for that fight. Shotgun Sheldon comes to mind. Ali would lie on the ropes while Sheldon hit him a hundred punches to the belly — that was Ali conditioning stomach and ribs to take Liston's pounding. In that direction lay his duty, but his pleasure was by way of sparring with Ellis as if Ali had no need to study Sonny's style when he could elaborate the wit and dazzle of his own.

Fighters generally use a training period to build confidence in their reflexes, even as an average skier, after a week of work on his parallel, can begin to think he will yet look like an expert. In later years, however, Ali would concentrate less on building his own speed and more on how to take punches. Now, part of his art was to reduce the force of each blow he received to the head and then fraction it further. Every fighter does that, indeed a young boxer will not last long if his neck fails to swivel at the instant he is hit, but it was as if Ali were teaching his nervous system to transmit shock faster than other men could.

Maybe all illness results from a failure of communication between mind and body. It is certainly true of such quick disease as a knockout. The mind can no longer send a word to the limbs. The extreme of this theory, laid down by Cus D'Amato when managing Floyd Patterson and José Torres, is that a pugilist with an authentic desire to win cannot be knocked out if he sees the punch coming, for then he suffers no dramatic lack of communication. The blow may hurt but cannot wipe him out. In contrast, a five-punch combination in which every shot lands is certain to stampede any opponent into unconsciousness. No matter how light the blows, a jackpot has been struck. The sudden overloading of the victim's message center is bound to produce that inrush of confusion known as coma.

Now it was as if Ali carried the idea to some advanced place where he could assimilate punches faster than other fighters, could literally transmit the shock through more parts of his body, or direct it to the best path, as if ideally he were working toward the ability to receive that five-punch combination (or six or seven!) yet be so ready to ship the impact out to each arm, each organ and each leg, that the punishment might be digested, and the mind remain clear. It was a study to watch Ali take punches. He would lie on the ropes and paw at his sparring partner like a mother cat goading her kitten to belt away. Then Ali would flip up his glove and let the other's punch bounce from that glove off his head, repeating the move from other angles, as if the second half of the art of getting hit was to learn the trajectories with which punches glanced off your gloves and still hit you; Ali was always studying how to deaden such shots or punish the glove that threw the punch, forever elaborating his inner comprehension of how to trap, damp, modify, mock, curve, cock, warp, distort, deflect, tip, and turn the bombs that came toward him, and do this with a minimum of movement, back against the ropes, languid hands up. He invariably trained by a scenario that cast him as a fighter in deep fatigue, too tired to raise his arms in the twelfth round of a fifteen-round fight. Such training may have saved him from being knocked out by Frazier in their first fight, such training had been explored by him in every fight since. His corner would scream "Stop playing!," the judges would score against him for lying on the ropes, the fight writers would report that he did not look like the old Ali and all the while he was refining methods.

This afternoon, however, in Deer Lake it looked as if he were learning very little. He was getting hit by stupid punches and they seemed to take him by surprise. He was not languid but sluggish. He looked bored. He showed, as he worked, all the sullen ardor of a husband obliging himself to make love to his wife in the thick of carnal indifference.

The first sparring partner, Larry Holmes, a young light-colored Black with a pro record of nine wins and no losses, boxed aggressively for three rounds, hitting Ali more often than he got hit in return, which in itself might not have been unusual — sometimes Ali would not throw a punch through all of a round — but on this afternoon it seemed as if Ali did not know how to use Holmes. Ali had the disgusted expression Sugar Ray Robinson used to get toward the end of his career when struck on the nose, a grimace of disdain for the occupation as if you could lose your looks if you weren't careful. The afternoon was hot, the gym was even hotter. It was filled with tourists, more than a hundred, who had paid a dollar to get in — there was a late-summer apathy to the proceedings. Once in a while, Ali would set out to chastise Holmes for his impudence, but Holmes was not there to be instructed for nothing. He fought back with all the eagerness of a young pro who sees a maximum of future for himself. Ali could of course have given a lesson, but he was boxing in the depths of a bad mood. Part of Ali's strength in the ring was fidelity to his mood. If, when speaking to the press, a harsh and hysterical tone entered his voice as easily as other men light a cigarette, he was never frantic in the ring, at least not since the fight with Liston in Miami in 1964 when he won the Heavyweight Championship. No, just as Marlon Brando seemed to inhabit a role as though it were a natural extension of his mood, so Ali treated boxing. In a bad mood, he would stay in his lethargy, box out of his very distaste for the staleness of this occupation. Often he trained all of an afternoon in such a bad spirit. The difference today was that he was running into unexpected punches — the end of the world for Ali. In annoyance, he would punish Holmes by wrapping an arm around his head. Over the years, Ali had become one of the best wrestlers in the ring. But then if karate kicks had been introduced to boxing, Ali would also have been first at that. His credo had to be that nothing in boxing was foreign to him. Now, however, such virtuosity was reduced to wrestling with Holmes. When they separated, Holmes would go back to the attack. Toward the end of three rounds, Ali started stinging him with punches. Holmes stung him back.

Ali's next sparring partner, Eddie "Bossman" Jones, a Light-Heavyweight, was a dark sawed-off version of George Foreman. He didn't look five-ten in height, and Ali used him as a playmate. Absolutely comfortable with Jones (a fighter reminiscent of other fighters who stood flat-footed and belted away) Ali lay on the ropes and took Bossman's punches when he chose to and blocked them when he wished. For all it seemed to demand, Ali could have been an inspector on an assembly line, accepting and rejecting the product. "This piece passes, this one won't." To the degree that boxing is carnality, meat against meat, Ali was master when it was time to receive, he got the juice out of it, the aesthetic juice of the punches he blocked or slipped, plus all the libidinal juice of Bossman Jones banging away on his gut. For all of a round Bossman belabored Ali, and Ali communed with himself. In the second of their two rounds, Ali stepped off the ropes for the last two minutes and proceeded for the first time in the afternoon to throw punches. His master's assortment leaped forth, jabs with a closed glove, jabs with an open fist, jabs with a twist of the glove to the right, jabs with a turn to the left, then a series of right-hand leads offered like jabs, then uppercuts and easy hooks from a stand-up position, full of speed off both hands. With each punch, his glove did something different, as if the fist and wrist within the glove were also speaking.

Now, Ali's trainer, Bundini, came alive with cries from

the corner. "All night long!" he shouted happily. But Ali did not throw anything hard, rather he hit Bossman Jones with a pepperpot, ting, ting, bing, bap, bing, ting, bap! and Bossman's head bapped back and forth like a speed bag. "All night long!" There was something obscene in watching, as if the man's head were on a potter's wheel and into a speed bag precisely was it being shaped. Although he had not been hit with any force, Jones (one score for the theorem of D'Amato) was wobbly when the round ended. And happy. He had been good for the boss. He had the kind of face to propose that thousands of punches had bounced off his persona, that celestial glow of a hard worker whose intelligence has been pounded out long ago.

The last three rounds were with Roy Williams, introduced to the crowd as Heavyweight Champion of Pennsylvania, and he was Ali's size, a dark gentle sleepy-looking man who boxed with such respect for his employer that the major passion appeared to be a terror of messing Ali's charisma. Williams pawed the air and Ali wrestled him around. He seemed to be working now more on wrestling than boxing, as if curious to test his arms against Roy Williams's strength. Three slow rounds went by with the head of the Heavyweight Champion of Pennsylvania in the crook of Ali's bicep. It looked like the terminal stage of a street fight when not much more than heavy breathing will go on.

Ali had now been boxing eight rounds, five of them easy, too easy to show this much fatigue — the green of his skin did not speak of a good liver. The tourists, a crowd in the main of white mill workers in flowered sport shirts, sprinkled with an occasional beard or biker, looked apathetic. You had to be familiar with Ali's methods to have even a remote idea of what this workout could signify. Toward the middle of the last round Bundini began to be heard again. Hardly unknown to readers of sports columns (for he was the inventor of "Float like a butterfly, sting like a bee") he had on average days a personality more intense per cubic inch than Ali's, and was now screaming in a voice every onlooker would remember, for it was not only hoarse and imprecatory but suggestive of the ability to cut through every insulation in the atmosphere. Bundini was summoning djinns. "Snake-whip him! Stick him! Stick mean!" he howled with his head back, his bald rocketing eyes spearing ectoplasmic ogres. Ali did not respond. He and Roy Williams kept clinching, wrestling, and occasionally thumping one another. No art. Just the heavy exertions of overtired fighters so much like the lurching of overtired furniture movers. "Get *off*," cried Bundini, "get *off* on him." Seconds were ticking down. Bundini wanted a flurry, wanted it for morale, for Ali's good conscience tonight, for the confirming of good habit, for the end if nothing else of this wretched bad mood. "Get off on him! Stick him! Come on, baby. Let's close the show on him, *let's close this show!* Get *off*. Close him! Close him! *Close him!*" went Bundini into the final hollering seconds of the eighth and final round and Ali and Williams, working slowly, came to the end of their day. No dervish. No flurry. The bell. It was not a happy workout. Ali looked sour and congested.

He did not look a great deal happier one hour later when available for interview. He sprawled on a couch in his dressing room, the exertion of the workout still on him, so that he looked heavy for once and not intelligent; indeed, not even handsome. His face was a hint swollen. It offered the suggestion his head would thicken, and he would look more like a pug in years to come. Most startling was his lack of energy. Usually Ali liked to talk after a workout, as though the physical effort only teased his energies enough to confirm his passion, which was to speak. Today, however, he lay back on the couch, let others talk to him. There were a number of Black men in the room, and they approached as courtiers, each taking his turn to whisper in Muhammad's ear, then falling back to sit in audience. An interviewer from a Black network held a microphone ready in case Ali wished to respond, but this was one occasion when he did not.

The workout seemed to have taken too much. An absence of stimulation heavy as gloom was in the air. Of course, it is not uncommon for fighters' camps to be gloomy. In heavy training fighters live in dimensions of boredom others do not begin to contemplate. Fighters are supposed to. The boredom creates an impatience with one's life, and a violence to improve it. Boredom creates a detestation for losing. So the furniture is invariably every shade of dull gray and dull brown, the sparring partners beaten half into insensibility are quiet when not morose, and the silence seems designed to prepare the fighter for his torture on the night of the fight. Ali's camps, however, usually offered vivacity, his own if no one else's. It was as if Ali insisted on having fun while he trained. Not today. It was like any fighter's camp. Unspoken sentiments of defeat passed through the drably furnished room.

Just as a man serving a long sentence in prison will begin to live in despair about the time he recognizes that the effort to keep his sanity is going to leave him less of a man, so a fighter goes through something like the same calculation. The prisoner or the fighter must give up some part of what is best in him (since what is best for any human is no more designed for prison — or training — than an animal for the zoo). Sooner or later the fighter recognizes that something in his psyche is paying too much for the training. Boredom is not only deadening his personality but killing his soul. No surprise then if Ali had been in revolt against training for half a career.

"What do you think of the odds?" someone asked, and the question, thrown up without preparation, left Ali looking out-of-phase. "I don't know about betting," he said. It was explained that man-to-man the odds were 2½ to 1 against him. "That's a lot?" he asked, and said almost in surprise, "They really think Foreman'll win!" He looked less depressed for the first time this day. "You fellows are in position to make a lot of money with odds like that." Thought of the fight, however, seemed to cheer him a faint degree as if he were a convict thinking of the hour when his time is up. (Of course a killer might be waiting on the street.) "Would you like," he asked on the spur of this small cheer, "to hear my new poem?"

No one in the room had the heart to say no. Ali motioned to a flunky who brought up a purse from which the fighter extracted a sheaf of worked-over pages, handling this literature with the same concentration of his fingertips a poor man brings to counting off a roll of cash. Then he began to read. The Blacks listened with piety, their eyes off on calculations to the side.

"I have," said Ali, "a great one-two punch."

"The one hits a lot, but the two hits a bunch."

Everybody snickered. The lyric went on to suggest that Ali was sharp as a razor and Foreman might get cut.

"When you look at him he will make you sick,

"Because on his face, you will see nick after nick."

Ali finally put the pages away. He waved a hand at the obedient mirth. The poem had been three pages. "How long did it take to write?" he was asked. "Five hours," he replied — Ali who could talk at the rate of three hundred new words a minute. Since the respect was for the man, for all of the man including the literary talent (just as one might be ready to respect the squeaks Balzac could elicit from a flute if that would prove revelatory of one nerve in Balzac — one nerve, anyway), so came an image of Ali, pencil in hand, composing down there in the depths of Black reverence for rhyme — those mysterious links in the universe of sound: no rhyme ever without its occult reason! Did Ali's rhymes help to shape the disposition of the future, or did he just sit there after a workout and slowly match one dumb-wit line to the next?

Ali's psychic powers were never long removed, however, from any critical situation. "That stuff," he said, waving his hands, "is just for fun. I got serious poetry I'm applying my mind to." He looked interested for the first time this day in what he was doing. Now from memory he recited in an earnest voice:

> *The words of truth are touching*
> *The voice of truth is deep*
> *The law of truth is simple*
> *On your soul you reap.*

It went on for a good number of lines, and finally ended with, "The soul of truth is God," an incontestable sentiment to a Jew, Christian, or Muslim, incontestable indeed to anyone but a Manichean like our interviewer. But then the interviewer was already worrying up another aesthetic street. The poem could not possibly be original. Perhaps it was a translation of some piece of devotional Sufi that Ali's Muslim teachers read to him, after which he might have changed a few of the words. Still, a certain line stayed: "On your soul you reap." Had one really heard it? Could he have written it? In all of Ali's twelve years of prophetic boxing doggerel — the poem as worthless as the prediction was often exact: Archie Moore/ is sure/ to hug the floor/ by the end of four — some such scheme! — this line must be the first example in Ali's voluminous canon of an idea not resolutely antipoetic. For Ali to compose a few words of real poetry would be equal to an intellectual throwing a good punch. Inquiries must be made. Ali, however, could not remember the line out of context. He had to recall the entire poem. Only his memory was not working. Now one felt the weight of punches he had taken this afternoon. Line by line his voice searched aloud for the missing words. It took five minutes. It became in that time another species of endeavor as if the act of recollection might also restore some of the circuits disarranged in the brain that day. With all the joy of an eight-year-old child exhibiting good memory in class, Ali got it back at last. Patience was rewarded. "The law of truth is simple. As you sow, you reap."

As you sow, you reap! Ali's record was intact. He had still to write his first line of poetry.

The exercise, nonetheless, had awakened him. He began to talk of Foreman, and with gusto. "They think he's going to beat me?" Ali cried aloud. As if his sense of the universe had been offended, he said with wrath, "Foreman's nothing but a hard-push puncher. He can't *hit!* He's never knocked a man out. He had Frazier down six times, couldn't knock him out. He had José Roman, a nobody, down four times, couldn't knock him out! Norton down four times! That's not a puncher. Foreman just pushes people down. He can't give me trouble, he's got no left hook! Left hooks give me trouble. Sonny Bates knocked me down with a left hook, Norton broke my jaw, Frazier knocked me down with a left hook, but Foreman — he just got slow punches, take a year to get there." Now Ali stood up and threw round air-pushing punches at the air. "You think that's going to bother *me?*" he asked, throwing straight lefts and rights at the interviewer that filled the retina two inches short. "This is going to be the greatest upset in the history of boxing." Ali was finally animated. "I have an inch and a half over him in reach. That's a lot. Even a half-inch is an advantage, but an inch and a half is a lot. That's a lot."

It was not unknown that a training camp was designed to manufacture one product — a fighter's ego. In Muhammad's camp, however, it was not the absent manager, nor the trainers, nor the sparring partners, nor certainly the

gloomy ambience of the camp itself which did the manu-
facturing. No, the work was done by Ali. He was the product of his own raw material. There was no chance for
Foreman as he stated his case. Still, memories stirred of
Foreman's dismantlement of Ken Norton in two rounds.
That night, commenting at ringside just after the fight, Ali's
voice had been shrill. When he started to talk to the TV
interviewers his first remark — uncharacteristic of Ali —
was, "Foreman can hit harder than me." If Ali had made
excuses to himself for his own two long even fights with
Norton, such excuses had just been ripped out of his ego.
In Caracas that night, directly before his eyes, he had seen
a killer. Foreman had been vicious like few men ever seen
in the ring. In the second round, as Norton started to go
down for the second time, Foreman caught him five times,
as quick in the instant as a lion slashing its prey. Maybe
Foreman couldn't hit, but he could execute. That instant
must have searched Ali's entrails.

Of course, a great fighter will not live with anxiety like
other men. He cannot begin to think of how much he can
be hurt by another fighter. Then his imagination would not
make him more creative but less — there is, after all, endless anxiety available to him. Here at Deer Lake, the order
was to bury all dread; in its place Ali breathed forth a bale-
ful self-confidence, monotonous in the extreme. Once again
his charm was lost in the declamation of his own worth and
the incompetence of his enemy. Yet his alchemy functioned.
Somehow, buried anxiety was transmuted to ego. Each day
interviewers came, each day he learned about the 2½–1
odds for the first time, and subjected his informants to the

same speech, read the same poems, stood up, flashed punches two inches short of their face. If reporters brought tape recorders to capture his words, they could end with the same interview word for word even if their visits were a week apart. One whole horrendous nightmare — Foreman's extermination of Norton — was being converted, reporter by reporter, poem by poem, same analysis after same analysis — "He's got a hard-push punch but he can't *hit*" — into the reinstallation of Ali's ego. The funk of terror was being compressed into psychic bricks. What a wall of ego Ali's will had erected over the years.

Before leaving, there is an informal tour of the training camp. Deer Lake is already famous in the media for its replicas of slave cabins high on Ali's hill and the large boulders painted with the names of his opponents, Liston's name on the rock you see first from the entrance road. Each return to camp has to remind Ali of these boulders. Once these names were fighters to stir panic in the middle of sleep and a chill on awakening. Now they are only names, and the cabins please the eye, Ali's most of all. Its timbers are dark with the hue of the old railroad bridge from which they were removed; the interior, for fair surprise, is kin to a modest slave cabin. The furniture is simple but antique. The water comes from a hand pump. An old lady with the manners of a dry and decent life might seem the natural inhabitant of Ali's cabin. Even the four-poster bed with the patchwork quilt seems more to her size than his own. Outside the cabin, however, the philosophical residue of this old lady is obliterated by a hard-top parking area. It is larger than a basketball court, and all the buildings, large and small, abut it. How much of Ali is here. The subtle taste of the Prince of Heaven come to lead his people collides with the raucous blats of Muhammad's media sky where the only firmament is asphalt and the stars give off glints in the static.

2. THE BUMMER

WITNESS ANOTHER Black man's taste: It is the Presidential
Domain of President Mobutu at Nsele on the banks of the
Congo, a compound of white stucco buildings with roads
that extend over a thousand acres. A zoo can be found in
some recess of its grounds and an Olympic swimming pool.
There is a large pagoda at the entrance, begun as a gift
from the Nationalist Chinese, but completed as a gift by
the Communist Chinese! We are in a curious domain:
Nsele! It extends from the highway to the Congo over fields
in cultivation, two miles to the Congo, now called the Zaïre,
the enormous river here a disappointment for its waters are
muddy and congested with floating clumps of hyacinth
ripped loose from the banks and thick as carcasses in the
water, unromantic as turds. A three-decker riverboat, hy-
brid between yacht and paddle steamer, is anchored at the
dock. The boat is called *President Mobutu*. Next to it, similar in appearance, is a hospital ship. It is called *Mama
Mobutu*. No surprise. The posters that advertise the fight
say "*Un cadeau de President Mobutu au peuple Zairois*"

(a gift of President Mobutu to the Zairois people) *"et un honneur pour l'homme noir"* (plus an honor for the Black man). Like a snake around a stick, the name of Mobutu is intertwined in Zaïre with the revolutionary ideal. "A fight between two Blacks in a Black nation, organized by Blacks and seen by the whole world; that is a victory for Mobutism." So says one of the government's green and yellow signs on the highway from Nsele to the capital, Kinshasa. A variety of such signs printed in English and French give the motorist a whiz-by-the-eye course in Mobutism. "We want to be free. We don't want our road toward progress to be impeded; even if we have to forge our way through rock, we will forge it through the rock." It is better than Burma Shave and certainly a noble sentiment for the vegetation of the Congo, but the interviewer is thinking that after much travel he has come to an unattractive place. Of course, the interviewer is also looking green. He has caught some viral disruption in Cairo before coming to Zaïre and has only been in this country for three miserable days. He will even leave for New York just this afternoon. The fight has been postponed. Foreman has been cut in training. Since it is over the eye, the postponement, while indefinite, can hardly be less than a month. What a bummer! The day he landed in Zaïre was the day he heard the news. His hotel reservations had, of course, been unhonored. There is nothing like failing to find a bed when you land at dawn in an African capital. Much of the morning was lost before he was finally assigned a room at the Memling, famous for its revolutionary history. A decade ago, correspondents lived on its upper stories at a time when protagonists were being executed in the lobby. Blood ran over the lobby floor. But now the Memling looked like itself once more, a mediocre hotel in a tropical town. The famous floor of the lobby was more or less equal again in cleanliness and good feeling to the floor of the Greyhound bus station in Easton, Pennsylvania, and the natives at the desk spoke French like men with artificial larynxes. They were nonetheless as superior in their attitude toward foreigners as any Parisian. What pride in the inability to comprehend your accent! What a lobby to be executed in! The Zairois officials who passed through these precincts wore dark blue lapelless jackets and matching blue pants called *aboscos* (from the slogan *"à bas le costume"* — down with formal dress) and that was the approved bureaucratic revolutionary wear. Since some of these officials even spoke English (with accents more tortured than the Japanese — words catapulting from their gut as they popped their eyes) irritation teemed in every dialogue. Between white and Black, arrogance massed against arrogance. The decision of the press was that the Zairois had to be the rudest people in Africa. Quickly, relations between Zairois and visiting whites became mutual detestations. To obtain what one desired, whether a drink, a room, or an airline ticket, a surly Belgian tone was the peremptory voice to offer. If, for example, you hung up the phone after waiting twenty minutes for an answer, be certain the hotel operator would call back to revile you for discommoding him. Then one had to get into the skin of a *cultivateur Belgique* defining reality to plantation hands. *"La connection était im . . . par . . . faite!"* Manners became so bad that American Blacks were snarling at African Blacks. What a country of old knots and new.

Worse than that. To be in the Congo for the first time

21

and know its name had been changed. More debilitating than cannibalism was this contribution to anomie. To reach the edge of the "Heart of Darkness," here at the old capital of Joseph Conrad's *horror*, this Kinshasa, once evil Leopoldville, center of slave trade and ivory trade, and to see it through the bilious eyes of a tortured intestine! Was it part of Hemingway's genius that he could travel with healthy insides? Who had ever wanted so much to be back in New York? If there were charms to Kinshasa, where to find them? The center of town had all the panache of an inland Florida city of seventy or eighty thousand people who somehow missed their boom — a few big buildings looked at a great many little ones. But Kinshasa did not have eighty thousand people. It had a million, and it ran for forty miles around a bend of the Congo, now, yes, the Zaïre. It was no more agreeable than passing through forty miles of truck traffic and car-stained suburbs around Camden or Biloxi. If there was an inner city full of squalor and color called La Cité where natives lived in an endless tumbledown of creeks, lurching dirt roads, nightclubs, wall shops and hovels, our traveler was still too queasy with the internal mismanagement of his life to pay a visit, and thought only of getting home. Of course, living in such duress, the bile-producing emotions proved most satisfactory. What pleasure in the observation that this Black one-party revolutionary state had managed to couple some of the oppressive aspects of communism with the most reprehensible of capitalism. President Mobutu, the seventh (by repute) wealthiest man in the world, had decreed that the only proper term for one Zairois to use in addressing another was "Citoyen." On his average per-capita income of $70 a year, a Zairois, any Zairois, could still say "Citizen" to the seventh wealthiest man in the world. Small wonder then if the interviewer detested the Presidential Domain. These little white villas (reserved for the press) and the large white Congressional Hall (reserved for the training of the fighters) were a Levittown-on-the-Zaïre. Stucco buildings painted the color of aspirin were set behind lacy decorative open-air walls reminiscent of the worst of Edward Durrell Stone, a full criticism — since even the best of Edward Durrell Stone is equal to taking a cancer pill — no, this pretentious Nsele with its two-mile drive and its hordes of emaciated workers in the watermelon fields (one could pass a thousand Blacks on the road before one glimpsed a man with the faintest suggestion of girth) was a technological confection equal to NASA or Vacaville, a minimum-security prison for the officers of the media and the visiting bureaucrats of the world. One high white and chromium tower with the initials of the party — MPR — stood up as a pillar to mass phallic rectitude. It was a long way from Joseph Conrad and the old horror. Maybe it took a mind as extreme as his own to be ready to argue that the plastic niceties of Edward Durrell Stone were still equal in odium to the Belgian Congo of 1880:

They were not enemies, they were not criminals, they were nothing earthly now — nothing but black shadows of disease and starvation, lying confusedly in the greenish gloom. Brought from all the recesses of the coast in all the legality of time contracts, lost in uncongenial surroundings, fed on unfamiliar food, they sickened, became inefficient, and were then allowed to crawl away and rest. These moribund shapes were free as air — and nearly as thin. I began to distinguish the gleam of the eyes under the trees. Then, glancing down, I saw a face near my hand. The black bones reclined at full length with one shoulder against the tree, and slowly the eyelids rose and the sunken eyes looked up at me, enormous and vacant, a kind of blind, white flicker in the depths of the orbs, which died out slowly. The man seemed young — almost a boy — but you know with them it's hard to tell. I found nothing else to do but to offer him one of my good Swede's ship's biscuits I had in my pocket. The fingers closed slowly on it and held — there was no other movement and no other glance.

At Nsele, Ali was ensconced in a villa just across the street from the banks of the Zaïre. The interior of his house had been furnished by the government in style one might expect. Large rooms twice the size of motel rooms but identically depressing in mood commanded the air. Long sofas and chairs were covered in green velveteen, the floor was a plastic gray tile, the cushions were orange, the table dark brown — one was looking at that ubiquitous hotel furniture known to the wholesale trade as High Schlock.

It was nine in the morning. Ali had been sleeping. If he looked better than at Deer Lake, the hint of a lack of full health still lingered. In fact, there had been news stories that his blood sugar was low, his energy poor, and he had been placed on a new diet. Still, there was no large improvement in his appearance.

This morning he was twice depressed over Foreman's

cut. The fight had been hardly a week away. A TV corre-
spondent, Bill Brannigan, who spoke to Ali just after he
heard the news, was to remark, "It's the first time I ever
saw Ali have a genuine reaction." How he was upset. "The
worst of all times," said Ali, "and the worst thing that could
have happened. I feel as if somebody close to me just died."
Could it be the developing determination of his body that
had just died, his difficult approach to good condition? But
even to speak of good condition is to confront the first mys-
tery of boxing. It is a rare state of body and mind that al-
lows a Heavyweight to move at top speed for fifteen rounds.
That cannot be achieved by an act of will. Yet Ali had been
trying. For months he had trained.

The irony was that there had been a time when he was
always in such shape. Before his second fight with Liston,
you could catch him in the middle of any gymnasium session and he was superb. His body could not betray him.
You would define happiness by his estimate of his own condition. But that was a decade ago. In the three years after
his title was taken for refusing to go into the army — "No
Viet Cong ever called me 'Nigger' " — he had every kind of
life but a fighter's; he lectured, was onstage in New York
as an actor, traveled, lay fallow. He had fun. Ever since, he
trained with an eye for the fun he would have just so soon
as training each day was done. On the night before his first
Norton fight, hands aching with arthritis, his ankle injected
with cortisone, he went nonetheless to a party. The next
night, Norton broke his jaw. Afterward Ali forced himself
to train a little harder, but it was the chore of his life. Only
for the second Frazier fight and now for Foreman had he

been ready to submit to the depressing grind of trying to get into top condition. How many months had he labored at Deer Lake! And even ate fish for his arthritis and avoided meat. His hands healed. He could hit the heavy bag again. But then his energy diminished. After that long season of training, his energy still diminished! Something in the cosmic laws of violence must be carnal and command you to eat meat. So he had given up fish, resumed the flesh of animals, ate desserts, and his blood sugar came back. He might even be ready at last to enter the fight which would test the logic of his life. Now the postponement must have felt like an amputation. What a danger. Every cell in his body could be ready to mutiny.

He was, however, philosophical on this morning forty-eight hours later. "A real disappointment," he said, "a real disappointment. But Allah has revealed to me that I must look on this as my *private* lesson in disappointment. This is my opportunity to learn how to convert the worst of disappointment into the greatest of strength. For the seed of triumph can be found in the *misery* of the disappointment. Allah has allowed me to see this postponement as a blessing," said Ali, and finger in the air, added, "The greatest surprise is always to be found in one's own heart."

Only Ali could make this speech at nine in the morning and lead you to believe he believed it. "Nonetheless," said Ali, "it is *hard*. I am tired of training. I want to eat all the apple cobbler and drink all the sweet cream." Then — was it because they were standing through this speech? — the interviewer was now formally introduced to Ali's Black associates as "a great writer. No'min is a man of wisdom," said Ali. A serious hindrance to the interview. For after such an introduction how can Ali not wish to read his poetry? In turn, a man of wisdom may wish to be courageous but obliged to face such verse, he will take up the cult of the craven. How No'min dodges Ali's desire for a critique on the poems. Every literary principle is swallowed as Ali recites — it is equal in aesthetic sin to applauding the design of Nsele.

Once again, however, the poetry is not doggerel but derives from Ali's mysterious source. From a sheaf of some hundred pages, each page so covered by his large handwriting that not fifty words make a page, Ali speaks of the heart. It is a curious poem. Again, it is difficult to decide how much of the language is his own, but it is certainly a poem on the nature of the heart. He declaims it like a sermon, sounding indeed like a bright thirteen-year-old admired for the ability to stand at the altar and speak as loud as a grown-up. The poem explores the categories of heart. There is the heart of iron which must be put into the fire before any change can be made in it, and the heart of gold which reflects the glory of the sun. As one's attention begins to wander, so one only hears in passing of hearts of silver and copper and rock and the craven heart of wax which melts before heat (although it can be given any useful shape by superior intention). Then Ali speaks of "the heart of paper that flies like a kite in the wind. One can control the heart of paper as long as the string is strong enough to hold it. But when there is no wind, it drops."

A diversion is attempted. It is suggested that Ali must have a heart of iron. Ali shows surprise. He sees himself with a heart of gold. Now silence follows the reading.

"These are fine sermons," Norman says. "When you take

up a career as a minister, they will be perfect for what you want to do." His intestines punish him immediately for such hypocrisy. Moreover, this lack of direct comment does not improve Ali's mood. It turns into a morning without focus. Since there will be no training later today, Ali is restless. "Maybe I will warm up a little," he says. "These people in Africa like to see me, and the postponement has been a shock for them. Maybe it'll relieve their feelings if they see I am still training."

"Do you intend to stay here until the fight?"

"Oh, I have no desire to move. My place is here with my people." There had been rumors that neither Ali nor Foreman were being allowed to leave Zaïre. It was certain at any rate that soldiers surrounded Foreman's villa. In the hour after the Champion was cut, Mobutu's man in Nsele, Bula Mandungu, tried to keep the story quiet, only to discover that word had already gone out to America from the one Telex machine his assistants had neglected to put out of order. Bula, whose small eyes offered the small welcome of a man who has packed a holster on his hip for twenty years, now scolded the press. "You must not publicize this," he said. "It will be improperly understood in your country. I suggest you forget about such a story. The cut is nothing. Go for a swim. Foreman should be able to train again tomorrow." Bula had put in three years in East Germany and four in Moscow, which may have given him his conversational style. "Americans are hysterical," he said. "They always dramatize things."

A brave official in the State Department now loaned his black American Embassy limousine to a few reporters so they might drive to Foreman's villa four miles away. But, on arrival the reporters were not allowed to get out of the car. On the porch, Foreman's manager, Dick Sadler, kept waving for them to come up and visit, but the security man who halted the car was quick to say, "You are bothering the Champion."

"We're not. Can't you see that his manager is waving to us," said John Vinocur of the Associated Press.

"You are bothering *me*," said the security man, and signaled to his security guards. They now came forward with Uzi submachine guns, product of an old flirtation with the Israelis. Since Mobutu had also been known for his Nationalist and Communist Chinese pagoda, his private homes in Belgium, Paris, and Lausanne, his Swiss banks, his current Arab flirtation, and the remarkable good favor of the CIA in Kinshasa, who were reputed to have pulled off the coup which first brought him power, it was not unfair to think of the President of Zaïre as an eclectic. (Truth: he was one centerpiece of an eclectic!) The reporters paid their respects to such virtuosity by withdrawing this official American limousine with its attached American flag from the Israeli Uzis in the hands of the Black Mobutu security guard. Now the joke at press tables was that the U.S. Marines would have to bust into the Congo before Ali could be liberated.

But time passed uneventfully in the room with the High Schlock furniture. People came into the villa and went. Ali sat on one of the green velveteen chairs and gave an interview, then another. He analyzed Foreman's cut plus its effect on Foreman. "He's never been cut before. He used to think he was invincible. This has to hurt him." When analysis was satisfied, Ali went through an interview with an African reporter and expatiated on his intention to travel through the country of Zaïre after the fight. He spoke of his love for the Zairois people. "They are sweet and hardworking and humble and good people."

Time to go. If one would catch one's plane, it was time to say good-bye to Ali. So he sat down next to him, waited a minute, and said a few words of farewell. Maybe it was the thought of anybody's departure that produced the unexpected reply. Clearly, Ali muttered, "I gotta get out of this place."

Could the interviewer believe what he had heard? He leaned forward. This was as close as they had ever been. "Why don't you go on safari for a couple of days?"

With this remark, he lost the rest of his exclusive. Why hadn't he just said, "Yes, it's rough." Too late would he recognize that you approached Muhammad's psyche as carefully as you would walk up on a squirrel.

"No," said Ali, thrusting himself away from any temptation to scratch at the new itch, "I'll stay here and work for my people." Boxing is the exclusion of outside influence. A classic discipline.

Norman went back to the States with no happy intimations of the fight to come.

3. THE MILLIONAIRE

Now, OUR MAN of wisdom had a vice. He wrote about himself. Not only would he describe the events he saw, but his own small effect on events. This irritated critics. They spoke of ego trips and the unattractive dimensions of his narcissism. Such criticism did not hurt too much. He had already had a love affair with himself, and it used up a good deal of love. He was no longer so pleased with his presence. His daily reactions bored him. They were becoming like everyone else's. His mind, he noticed, was beginning to spin its wheels, sometimes seeming to repeat itself for the sheer slavishness of supporting mediocre habits. If he was now wondering what name he ought to use for his piece about the fight, it was out of no excess of literary ego. More, indeed, from concern for the reader's attention. It would hardly be congenial to follow a long piece of prose if the narrator appeared only as an abstraction: The Writer, The Traveler, The Interviewer. That is unhappy in much the way one would not wish to live with a woman for years and think of her as The Wife.

Nonetheless, Norman was certainly feeling modest on his return to New York and thought he might as well use his first name — everybody in the fight game did. Indeed, his head was so determinedly empty that the alternative was to do a piece without a name. Never had his wisdom appeared more invisible to him and that is a fair condition for acquiring an anonymous voice.

Back in Kinshasa, however, one month later, much was changed. Now, he had a good room at the Inter-Continental and so did every figure in Foreman's camp, the Champion, the manager, the sparring partners, the relatives, the friends, the skilled trainers — we are talking of no less than Archie Moore and Sandy Saddler — everyone in the retinue was there. Some of Ali's camp were registered as well, most notably Bundini, who later would have verbal wars in the lobby with Foreman's people. What wars! They must yet be described. The promoters of the fight stayed at the Inter-Continental, John Daly, Don King, Hank Schwartz. Big Black, the big conga drummer from Ali's camp, was here. Interviewed by a British reporter who asked him the name of his drum, he answered that it was a conga. The reporter wrote Congo. The Zairois censor changed it to Zaïre. Now Big Black could say in interviews that he played the Zaïres.

Yes, a different mood. The food was better at the Inter-Continental, so were the drinks. The lobby was moving with easy action between Black and white. Musicians left over from the festival four weeks before, operators at the fringe of the promotion, fight experts, hustlers, and even a few tourists mingled with passing African bureaucrats and

European businessmen. Employees, male and female, from the gambling casinos came by for a look and mingled with Peace Corps kids and corporation men from cartels. Dashikis, bush jackets, and pinstripe suits passed through the lobby. Public Relations was quick to speak of "Kinshasa's living room." It was most peculiarly an agreeable lobby, although the autumn brown and pastel orange in the carpets, wicker chairs, walls, lamps and sofas were not different from autumn brown at the Indianapolis Hilton or the Sheraton Albuquerque. It worked in Africa. A little creature comfort went a long way in Kinshasa. The fast elevators gave zap! The fried food was eggs! Taxis came quickly. Still, the happy action was a function of the flow in the lobby rather than the status of people gathered. Social arbiters of Heavyweight Championships would have gone blind looking for a face important enough to ignore. If on the night before the fight a few well-known names would finally arrive, Jim Brown, Joe Frazier and David Frost for three, the old celebrity of the fight crowd was absent. The fight cadre plus George Plimpton, Hunter Thompson, Budd Schulberg and himself made up the notables. Any notions of anonymity had to be discarded.

For these days Norman was being welcomed by Blacks. If Ali had introduced him as "a man of wisdom" — Ali who had seen him in a dozen circumstances over the years and never quite allowed that he was sure of the name — Foreman, in turn, said, "Yeah I've heard of you. You're the champ among writers." Don King presented him as "a great mind among us, a genius." Bundini, lying in his teeth, assured everyone, "No'min is even smarter than I am."

33

Archie Moore, whom No'min had long revered, was cordial at last. A sparring partner asked for an autograph.

What celebration. Being greeted this warmly on return to Africa, he felt delivered at last from the bowels of the bummer. The final traces of the miserable fever that kept him in bed for a week on his return to New York were now gone. He was happy to be back in Africa. What a surprise. Since he was not being read in this milieu nearly so much as praised, and since the Black American community with its curious unities of opinion, so much like psychic waves, was spreading a good word on him for no overt reason — no recent published work or extraliterary relation to Blacks half so close as books and articles he had done ten or fifteen years earlier — he came at last to realize the fair shape of the irony. Months ago, a story had gotten into the newspapers about a novel he was writing. His publishers were going to pay him a million dollars sight unseen for the book. If his candles had been burning low in the literary cathedral these last few years, the news story went its way to hastening their extinction. He knew that his much publicized novel (still nine-tenths to be written) would now have to be twice as good as before to overcome such financial news. Good literary men were not supposed to pick up *sums*. Small apples for him to protest in every banlieu and literary purlieu that his Boston publisher had not been laid low with a degenerative disease of the cortex but that the million was to be paid out as he wrote five to seven hundred thousand words, the equivalent of five novels. Since he was being rewarded only as he delivered the work, and had debts and a sizable advance already spent and five wives and seven children, plus a financial nut at present larger than his head, so the sum was not as large as it seemed, he explained — the million, you see, was nominal.

Well, the literary world was built on bad cess. For good cause. If no one would be in a hurry to forgive him unless his novel proved immense, then maybe that would force his work closer to such scope. He might have time, at least to parse it out.

Here in Africa, however, it was another tale. Since the word of his million hit the wire services, his name throughout the Black community had been *underlined*. No'min Million was a man who could make it by using his head. No rough stuff! He did not have to get hit in the head, nor hit on the side of *your* head. This man had to be the literary champ. To make a million without taking chances — show respect! To sign for a sum that Heavyweight champs had not been able to make until Muhammad Ali came along — why, the optimistic element of the Black community, looking now at every commercial horizon in America, began to gaze at writing. Hang around this man went the word. Something might rub off!

Once, he would have been miserable at being able to prosper from such values. But his love affair with the Black soul, a sentimental orgy at its worst, had been given a drubbing through the seasons of Black Power. He no longer knew whether he loved Blacks or secretly disliked them, which had to be the dirtiest secret in his American life. Part of the woe of the first trip to Africa, part of that irrationally intense detestation of Mobutu — even a photo of the President in his plump cheeks and horn-rimmed eyeglasses igniting invective adequate to a Harvard professor looking at an icon of Nixon — must be a cover for the rage he was feeling toward Blacks, any Blacks. Walking the streets of Kinshasa on that first trip while the black crowds moved about him with an indifference to his presence that succeeded in niggering him, he knew what it was to be looked upon as invisible. He was also approaching, if not careful, the terminal animosity of a Senior Citizen. How his hatred seethed in search of a justifiable excuse. When the sheer evidence of Africa finally overcame these newly bigoted senses (when a drive over miles of highway showed thousands of slim and probably hungry Zairois running like new slum inhabitants for overcrowded buses, and yet in some absolute statement of aesthetic, some imprimatur of the holy and final statement of the line of the human body, these Blacks could still show in silhouette, while standing in line for the bus, almost every one of those thousand slim dark Africans, an incorruptible loneliness, a stone mute dignity, some African dignity he had never seen on South Americans, Europeans, or Asiatics, some tragic magnetic sense of self as if each alone and all were carrying the continent like a halo of sorrow about their head) then it became impossible not to feel the unique life of Africa — even if Kinshasa was to the rain forest as Hoboken to Big Sur — yes, impossible not to sense what everyone had been trying to say about Africa for a hundred years, big Papa first on line: the place was so fucking sensitive! No horror failed to stir its echo a thousand miles away, no sneeze was ever free of the leaf that fell on the other side of the hill. Then he could no longer hate the Zairois or even be certain of his condemnation of their own Black oppressors, then his animosity switched a continent over to Black Americans with their arrogance, jive, ethnic put-down costumes, caterwauling soul, their thump-your-testicle organ sound and black new vomitous egos like the slag of all of alienated sewage-compacted heap U.S.A.; then he knew that he had not only come to report on a fight but to look a little more into his own outsized feelings of love and — could it be? — sheer hate for the existence of Black on earth.

No, he was hardly surprised when his illness flared on return to the States, and he went through a week and then ten days of total detestation of himself, a fever without fantasies, an illness without terror, for he felt as if his soul had expired or, worse, slipped away. It was enough of a warning to lay a message on him. He got up from bed with the determination to learn a little about Africa before his return, a healthy impulse that brought him luck (but then, do we not gamble with the unrecognized thought that a return of our luck signifies a return of our health?). After inquiries, he went to the University Place Book Shop in New York, an operative definition of the word *warren*, up on the eighth or ninth floor of a wheezing old office building below Fourteenth Street — the smell of the catacombs in its stones — to find at exit from the elevator a stack and excelsior of books, cartons and dust where a big blond clerk with scraggly sideburns working alone assured the new customer that he could certainly afford these many books being laid on him, since he had after all been given the million, hadn't he, a worthless excursion to describe if not for the fact that the clerk picked the books, the titles all unfamiliar. Would there be one paragraph of radium in all this geographical, political, historical sludge? His luck came in; not a paragraph but a book: *Bantu Philosophy* by Father Tempels, a Dutch priest who had worked as missionary in the Belgian Congo and extracted the philosophy from the language of the tribes he lived among.

Given a few of his own ideas, Norman's excitement was not small as he read *Bantu Philosophy*. For he discovered that the instinctive philosophy of African tribesmen happened to be close to his own. Bantu philosophy, he soon learned, saw humans as forces, not beings. Without putting it into words, he had always believed that. It gave a powerful shift to his thoughts. By such logic, men or women were more than the parts of themselves, which is to say more than the result of their heredity and experience. A man was not only what he contained, not only his desires, his memory, and his personality, but also the forces that came to inhabit him at any moment from all things living and dead. So a man was not only himself, but the karma of all the generations past that still lived in him, not only a human with his own psyche but a part of the resonance, sympathetic or unsympathetic, of every root and thing (and witch) about him. He would take his balance, his quivering place, in a field of all the forces of the living and the dead. So the meaning of one's life was never hard to find. One did one's best to live in the pull of these forces in such a way as to increase one's own force. Ideally, one would do it in harmony with the play of all forces, but the beginning of wisdom was to enrich oneself, enrich the *muntu* which was the amount of life in oneself, the size of the human being in oneself. Crazy. We are returned to the Calvinism of the chosen where the man with most possessions is chosen, the man of force and wealth. We are certainly in the ghetto where you do not invade another turf. We are allied to every pride of property and self-enrichment. Back to the primitive sinews of capitalism! Bantu philosophy, however, is not so primitive. It may offer a more sinister vision: maybe it is nobler. For if we are our own force, we are also a servant of the forces of the dead. So we have to be bold enough to live with all the magical forces at loose between the living and the dead. That is never free of dread. It takes bravery to live with beauty or wealth if we think of them as an existence connected to the messages, the curses, and the loyalties of the dead.

In the presence of a woman who is finely dressed, an African might do more than salute the increase of power that accrues to the woman with her elaborate gown. To his eye, she would also have taken on the force that lives in the gown itself, the *kuntu* of the gown. That has its own existence. It, too, is a force in the universe of forces. The gown is like the increment in power an actor feels when he enters his role, when he senses the separate existence of the role as it comes up to him, much as if it had been *out there* waiting for him in the dark. Then, it is as if he takes on some marrow of the forgotten caves. It is why certain actors must act or go mad — they can hardly live without the clarity of that moment when the role returns.

Here is a passage from *The Palm Wine Drunkard* by Amos Tutuola:

We knew "Laugh" personally on that night, because as every one of them stopped laughing at us, "Laugh" did not stop for two hours. As "Laugh" was laughing at us on that night, my wife and myself forgot our pains and laughed with him, because he was laughing with curious voices that we never heard before in our life . . . so if somebody continue to laugh with "Laugh" himself, he or she would lie or faint at once for long laughing, because laugh was his profession.

When laughter presents such power, what are we to make of the African's attitude toward lust, the inevitable *kuntu* of *fuck* — yes, every word will have its relation to the primeval elements of the universe. "The word," says a Dogon sage named Ogotemmêli, "is water and heat. The force that carries the word comes out of the mouth in a water vapor which is both water and word." Nommo is at once the name of the word and the spirit of water. So Nommo lives everywhere: in the vapor of the air and the pores of the earth. Since the word is equal to water, all things are effected by Nommo, the word. Even the ear becomes an organ of sex when Nommo enters: "The good word, as soon as it is received by the ear, goes directly to the sex organ where it rolls in the uterus. . . ."

What exhilaration! This small fine book, *Bantu Philosophy*, and then a larger work bursting with intellectual sweetmeats, *Muntu, the New African Culture* by Janheinz Jahn, is illumining his last hours in New York, his flight on the plane — a night and a day! — his second impressions of Kinshasa. It has brought him back to a recognition of his old love for Blacks — as if the deepest ideas that ever entered his mind were there because Black existed. It has also brought back all the old fear. The mysterious genius of these rude, disruptive, and — down to it! — altogether indigestible Blacks. What noise they still made to the remains of his literary mind, what hooting, screaming and shrieking, what promise of oblivion on the turn of a card.

How his prejudices were loose. So much resentment had developed for black style, black snobbery, black rhetoric, black pimps, superfly, and all that virtuoso handling of the ho. The pride Blacks took in their skill as pimps! A wrath at the mismanagement of his own sensual existence now sat on him, a sorrow at how the generosity of his mind seemed determined to contract as he grew older. He could not really bring himself to applaud the emergence of a powerful people into the center of American life — he was envious. They had the good fortune to be born Black. And felt a private fury at the professional complacency of Black self-pity, a whole rage at the rhythmic power of those hectoring voices, a resentment at last of their values, of that eternal emphasis on centrality — "I am the real rooster on this block, the most terrible cock, the baddest fist. I'm a *down* dude. You motherfuckers better know it."

Yet even as he indulged this envy, he felt a curious relief. For he had come to a useful recognition. When the American Black was torn out of Africa, he was ripped out of his philosophy as well. So his violence and his arrogance could be a fair subject for comprehension once more. One had only to think of the torture. Everything in African philosophy was of the root, but the philosophy had been uprooted.

What a clipped and overstimulated transplant was the American Negro. His view of life came not only from his livid experience in America but from the fragments of his lost African beliefs. So he was alienated not from one culture but from two. What idea could an Afro-American retain, then, of his heritage if not that each man seeks the maximum of force for himself? Since he lived in a field of human forces that were forever changing, and changing dramatically, even as the people he knew were killed or arrested or fell out on junk, so he had to assert himself. How else could he find life? The loss of vital force was pure loss, equal to less ego, less status, less purchase on the availability of beauty. By comparison to the American Black, a white Judeo-Christian could live through a loss of vital force and feel moral, unselfish, even saintly and an African could feel himself in balance among traditional forces. An African could support the weight of his obligation to his father because his father was one step nearer in the chain to God — that unbroken chain of lives going back to the source of creation. But the American Black was sociologically famous for the loss of his father.

No wonder their voices called attention to themselves! They spoke of a vital (if tense) force. A poor and uneducated man was nothing without that force. To the degree it lived inside him, he was full of capital, ego capital, and that was what he possessed. That was the capitalism of the poor American Black trying to accumulate more of the only wealth he could find, respect on his turf, the respect of local flunkies for the power of his soul. What a raw, searching, hustling, competitive capitalism. What a lack of profit. The establishment offered massive restraint for such massive fevers of the ego. No surprise if tribal life in America began to live among stone walls and drugs. The drug gave magnification of the sentiment that a mighty force was still inside oneself, and the penitentiary restored the old idea that man was a force in a field of forces. If the social contract of the African restraint had been tradition, the American Black with a political ideal was obliged instead to live with revolutionary discipline. As he endured in his stone walls it became a discipline as pulverizing to the soul as the search for condition of a boxer.

Bantu Philosophy proved a gift, but it was one a writer might not need. Not to comprehend the fight. There was now enough new intellectual baggage to miss the train. Norman would bring some of it along, and hope he was not greedy. For Heavyweight boxing was almost all black, black as Bantu. So boxing had become another key to revelations of Black, one more key to black emotion, black psychology, black love. Heavyweight boxing might also lead to the room in the underground of the world where Black kings were installed: what was Black emotion, Black psychology, Black love? Of course, to try to learn from boxers was a quintessentially comic quest. Boxers were liars. Champions were great liars. They had to be. Once you knew what they thought, you could hit them. So their personalities became masterpieces of concealment. There would be limits to what he could learn of Ali and Foreman by the aid of any philosophy. Still, he was grateful for the clue. Humans were not beings but forces. He would try to look at them by that light.

4. A GANG OF CHAMPS

TAKEN DIRECTLY, Foreman was no small representative of vital force. He came out from the elevator dressed in embroidered bib overalls and dungaree jacket and entered the lobby of the Inter-Continental flanked by a Black on either side. He did not look like a man so much as a lion standing just as erectly as a man. He appeared sleepy but in the way of a lion digesting a carcass. His broad handsome face (not unreminiscent of a mask of Clark Gable somewhat flattened) was neither friendly nor unfriendly, rather, it was alert in the way a boxer is in some part of him alert no matter how sleepy he looks, a heightening common, perhaps, to all good athletes, so that they can pick an insect out of the air with their fingers but as easily notice the expression on some friend in the thirtieth row from ringside.

Since Norman was not often as enterprising as he ought to be, he was occasionally too forward. Having barely arrived in Kinshasa again, he did not know you were not supposed to speak to Foreman in the lobby and advanced on him with a hand out. In this moment, Bill Caplan, who did Public Relations for Foreman, rushed up to the fighter. "He's just come in, George," said Bill Caplan, and made an introduction. Foreman now nodded, gave an unexpected smile, and proceeded to make his kind remark about a champ at writing, his voice surprisingly soft, as Southern as it was Texan. His eyes warmed, as if he liked the idea of writing — the news would soon come out that Foreman was himself working on a book. Then he made a curious remark one could think about for the rest of the week. It was characteristic of a great deal about Foreman. "Excuse me for not shaking hands with you," he said in that voice so carefully muted to retain his powers, "but you see I'm keeping my hands in my pockets."

Of course! If they were in pockets, how could he remove them? As soon ask a poet in the middle of writing a line whether coffee is taken with milk or cream. Yet Foreman made his remark in such simplicity that the thought seemed likable rather than rude. He was telling the truth. It was important to keep his hands in his pockets. Equally important to keep the world at remove. He lived in a silence. Flanked by bodyguards to keep, exactly, to keep handshakers away, he could stand among a hundred people in the lobby and be in touch with no one. His head was alone. Other champions had a presence larger than themselves. They offered charisma. Foreman had silence. It vibrated about him in silence. One had not seen men like that for thirty years, or was it more? Not since Norman worked for a summer in a mental hospital had he been near anyone who could stand so long without moving, hands in pockets, vaults of silence for his private chamber. He had taken care then of catatonics who would not make a gesture from one meal to the next. One of them, hands contracted into fists, stood in the same position for months, only to erupt with a sudden punch that broke the jaw of a passing attendant. Guards were always informing new guards that catatonics were the most dangerous of the patients. They were certainly the strongest. One did not need other attendants, however, to tell you. If a deer's posture in the forest can say, "I am vulnerable, irreplaceable, and soon destroyed," so the posture of a catatonic haunts the brain. "Provided I do not move," this posture says, "all power will come to me."

There was here, however, no question of wondering whether Foreman might be insane. The state of mind of a Heavyweight Champion is considerably more special than that. Not many psychotics could endure the disciplines of professional boxing. Still, a Heavyweight Champion must live in a world where proportions are gone. He is conceivably the most frightening unarmed killer alive. With his hands he could slay fifty men before he would become too tired to kill any more. Or is the number closer to a hundred? Indeed one reason Ali inspired love (and relatively little respect for his force) was that his personality invariably suggested he would not hurt an average man, merely dispose of each attack by a minimal move and go on to the next. Whereas Foreman offered full menace. In any nightmare of carnage, he would go on and on.

Prizefighters do not, of course, train to kill people at large. To the contrary, prizefighting offers a profession to men who might otherwise commit murder in the street. Nonetheless, the violence capable of being generated in a champion like Foreman is staggering to contemplate when brought to focus against another fighter. This violence, converted to a special skill, had won him the Championship by his thirty-eighth fight. Foreman had never been defeated. On the night he won the Championship, he had accumulated no less than thirty-five knockouts, the fights stopped on an average before the third round. What an unbelievable record that is! Ten knockouts in the first, eleven in the second, eleven in the third and fourth. No need to think of him as psychotic, rather, as a physical genius who employed the methods of catatonia (silence, concentration and immobility). Since Ali was a genius in wholly separate ways, one could anticipate the rarest war of all — a collision between different embodiments of divine inspiration.

The fight would then be a religious war. That was to Ali's advantage. Who could say Ali was without a chance in any religious war that took place in Africa? Norman had smiled when first hearing of the match, thinking of evil eyes, conjurors, and black psychological fields. "If Ali can't win in Africa," he remarked, "he can't win anywhere." The paradox, however, on meeting the Champion was that Foreman seemed more black. Ali was not without white blood, not without a lot of it. Something in his personality was cheerfully even exuberantly white in the way of a six-foot two-inch president of a Southern college fraternity. At times Ali was like nothing so much as a white actor who had put on too little makeup for the part and so was not wholly convincing as a Black, just one of eight hundred small contradictions in Ali, but Foreman was *deep*. Foreman could be mistaken for African long before Ali. Foreman was in communion with a muse. And *she* was also deep, some distant cousin of beauty, the muse of violence in all her complexity. The first desire of the muse of violence may be to remain serene. Foreman could pass through the lobby like a virile manifest of the walking dead, alert to everything, yet immune in his silence to the casual pollutions of everybody's vibrating handshaking hands. Foreman's hands were as separate from him as a kuntu. They were his instrument, and he kept them in his pockets the way a hunter lays his rifle back into its velvet case. The last Heavyweight reminiscent of Foreman had been Sonny Liston. He used to inspire fear in a man by looking at him, his bad humor over intrusion into the aura of his person seethed like smoke. His menace was intimate — he could bury a little man as quickly as a big one.

Foreman, by comparison, might as well have been a contemplative monk. His violence was in the halo of his serenity. It was as if he had learned the lesson Sonny had been there to teach. One did not allow violence to dissipate; one stored it. Serenity was the vessel where violence could be stored. So everyone around Foreman had orders to keep people off. They did. It was as if Foreman was preparing to defend himself against the thoughts of everyone alive. If he entered the arena, and all of Africa wanted him to lose, then his concentration would become the ocean of his protection against Africa. A formidable defense.

Watching him in training, impressions were confirmed. The literary champ of Kinshasa was only a boxing expert of sorts; of sorts, for example, was his previous knowledge of

Foreman. He had seen him once four years ago in the course of winning a dubious decision in ten rounds over Gregorio Peralta. Foreman looked slow and clumsy. Then he never saw Foreman again until the second round against Norton. Having arrived late at the theater, he saw nothing but the knockdowns in the second round. It was hardly a complete picture of Foreman.

But seeing him in the ring at Nsele, it was obvious George had picked up sophistication. Everything in his training pointed toward this fight. His manager, Dick Sadler, had been in boxing just about all of his life. Archie Moore and Sandy Saddler, together with Sugar Ray Robinson, were precisely the three fighters who provided the most brilliant examples of technique for Ali's developing gifts. Foreman was one champion, therefore, whose training was being designed by other champions; it gave an opportunity to watch how a few of the best minds in boxing might work.

Against the perils of Africa and mass hysteria, the antidote was already evident; silence and concentration. If Africa was not Ali's only weapon, psychology must be his next. Would he try to punish Foreman's vanity? No physical activity is so vain as boxing. A man gets into the ring to attract admiration. In no sport, therefore, can you be more humiliated. Ali would use every effort to make Foreman feel clumsy. If, at his most fearsome, Foreman looked and fought like a lion, he had, at his worst, a resemblance to an ox. So the first object of training was to work on Foreman's sense of grace. George was being taught to dance. While he was still happy in the fox-trot, and Ali was eras beyond the frug, monkey, or jerk, no matter, Foreman was now able to glide in the ring, and that was what he would need. Training began with a loosening-up procedure other fighters did not employ. Foreman stood in the center of the ring and meditated as a weird and extraordinary music began to play through the public address system. It was pop. As ambitious, however, as pop music could ever become; sounds reminiscent of Wagner, Sibelius, Moussorgsky and many an electronic composer were in the mix. Nature was awakening in the morning — so went one's first assumption of the theme — but what a piece of nature! Macbeth's witches encountered Wagner's gods on a spastic dawn. Demons abounded. Caves boiled vapors. Trees split with the scream of a broken bone. The ground wrenched. Boulders fell onto musical instruments. Into these sounds, lyrical as movie-music dew, the sun slowly rose, leaves shook themselves, and the sorrowful throbs of an aching soul full of vamping organ dumps and thumps fulfilled some hollow in the din.

Foreman was wearing red trunks, a white T-shirt, reddish headgear, and bright red gloves, a bloody contrast to the sobriety of his mood. As the music played, he began to make small moves with his elbows and fists, miniscule locked-up uppercuts that did not travel an inch, small flicks of his neck, blinks of his eye. Slowly he began to shift his feet, but in awkward steps. He looked like a giant beginning to move after a five-year sleep. Making no attempt to appear impressive, he went through a somnambulistic dance. Near to motionless, he yet evoked the muffled roars of that steamy nature waking up, waking up. All by himself in the ring with a bewildered press and a wholly silent audience of several hundred Africans, he moved as though transition to the full speed of boxing would have to use up its convoluted time. Some Heavyweights were known for how long it took them to get ready — Marciano used to shadowbox five rounds in the dressing room before a title bout — but Foreman's warm-up suggested that he could become connected again to reflexes in himself only by separating himself altogether from time.

Yet as the music became less of a tone poem to Hieronymous Bosch and more like hints of *Oklahoma!* coming through Moussorgsky — what sweets and sours! — Foreman's feet began to slide, his arms to parry imaginary blows. Moving forward, he shadowboxed, cutting off the ring, throwing punches harder at the unstoppable air, working into the woe of every heavy puncher when he misses target (for no punch disturbs the shoulder more than the one that does not connect — professionals can be separated from amateurs by the speed with which their torso absorbs that instant's loss of balance). Now, Foreman having passed at last through these stages, Sadler cut off the music, and Foreman came to the corner. Wholly remote, he stood there while Sadler carefully greased his face and forehead for the sparring to come. But he was already returned to the full melancholy of isolation and concentration.

He sparred a round with Henry Clark, not trying to hit hard but enjoying himself. His hands were fast and he held them well out in front, picking off punches with quick leonine cuffs of his mitts, then countering quickly with lefts and rights. He had much to learn about moving his head, but his feet were nimble. Clark, a cherubic-looking Black

Heavyweight with a reputation of his own (eighth-ranking Heavyweight Contender), was being handled with authority by Foreman. A favorite of the press (for he was friendly and articulate), Clark had been declaring Foreman's praises for weeks. "George does not hit like other fighters," he would say. "Even a punch on the arms leaves you feeling paralyzed, and that's with heavy gloves. Ali is a friend of mine, and I'm afraid he's going to get hurt. George is the most punishing human being I've ever been in with."

This afternoon, however, with the fight five days away, Foreman was not working to punish Clark (who was due to fight the semifinal with Roy Williams) but, instead, was working at wrestling. Henry would try to hold him, as Ali might, and Foreman would throw him off, or shove him back, then maneuver him to the ropes, where he would hit him lightly, back off, and practice the same solution again from the center of the ring. For whatever reason — perhaps because Clark, a big man, was not elusive enough to test Foreman's resources at cutting off the ring — Sadler stopped the sparring after a round and put in Terry Lee, a slim white Light-Heavyweight who had the rugged face of a construction worker but happened to be fast as a rabbit. For three rounds, Lee did an imitation of Ali, backing in a circle to the ropes, then quickly skipping in the other direction to escape George, who held the center of the ring. Terry Lee was not big enough to take Foreman's punches, and Foreman did not try to punish him, merely tapping Lee when he was caught, but Terry gave an exhibition nonetheless, bouncing off the ropes to feint in one direction, bouncing back to feint in the other, and then would scoot through any escape route available, circling away from one set of ropes only to be driven almost immediately to the next, where he would duck, slide, put his hands to his head, fall back against the ropes, spring out, feint, drop his hands, dart, and try to move away again, Foreman stalking him all the while with enjoyment, for his reflexes were growing faster and faster.

Meanwhile, Foreman was learning new tricks every step of the way. Once, Terry Lee, springing off the ropes, skipped under Foreman's arms like a small boy escaping his father, and the African audience at the rear of the hall roared with derision. Foreman looked unperturbed, even interested, as if he had just picked up a trick by being fooled, and in the next round when Lee tried it again, Foreman was there to block escape. Watching Terry's talented imitation of Ali, yet seeing how cleverly and often Foreman was eating up room on the ropes and herding him toward a corner, it seemed certain that if Ali wished to win, he would have to take more punishment than ever before in his career.

Having finished three rounds with Lee, Foreman came out of the ring to work on the speed bag. Then he jumped rope. He did this with nice movement of his feet, skipping in enjoyment to the voice of Aretha Franklin, who was singing "You Got a Friend in Jesus." This workout, from inception to rope-jumping, had been going on for forty-five minutes, the length with one-minute rests of a ten-round fight, and Foreman did not look the least bit tired. He was thriving on the jump rope, the soles of his feet tapping the floor with the éclat of a drummer using his sticks. Foreman was more than graceful now — he was lively with the sweetness of his footwork.

Dick Sadler, his manager, flat cap back on his big round black head, called a halt. "Ladies and gentlemen," he announced to the crowd, "that ends our episode for today. We'll be back tomorrow doing the same thing in the same way." He looked confirmed in a good mood.

Foreman was close to genial in a press conference that followed. Dressed in his embroidered bib overalls, he sat on a long table with the press around him and quietly refused to use a microphone. Since his voice was low it was a direct difficulty for the fifty reporters and cameramen gathered, but he was exercising territorial rights. His mood was his property, and he did not want a shriek from the feedback to go tearing through his senses. Instead, the mike once refused, and the reporters crowded together, he responded to questions with an easy intelligence, his soft Texas voice not without resonance. His replies gave a tasty skew to the mood, as if there were more he could always say but would not in order to preserve the qualities of composure and serenity — they were tasty too.

As Foreman spoke, one of his fifty interviewers — it must be our recent convert to African studies — was thinking of *Conversations with Ogotemmêli* by Mercel Griaule, a fine book. Ogotemmêli looked on the gift of speech as analogous to weaving since the tongue and teeth were a warp and woof on which the breath could serve as thread. Given reflection, the idea was not so unsound. What, after all, was conversation if not a psychic material to be stitched by the mind to other psychic cloth? If most conversations ended in rags, so did most textiles.

Foreman spoke with a real sense of the delicacy of what

he might be weaving, a fine tissue, strong in its economy, a true cloth to come out of an intelligent and uneducated man who happened to be Champion.

Samples:

Reporter: "Your eye looks all right to me, George."

Foreman: "Looks all right to me, too."

Reporter: "What do you think of your weight?"

Foreman: "Once you're a Heavyweight, your weight speaks for itself."

Reporter: "Do you think you'll knock him out?"

Foreman (in utter relaxation): "I would like to."

On the ripple of humor this created, Foreman offered a smile. When the next questioner wondered what he thought of fighting at 3 A.M., Foreman gave a longer reply. "Once you're in good condition," he said, "you're able to do a lot of things you're not able to ordinarily. Good condition makes you more flexible. I really have no concern about the hour."

"Ali claims he's met more tough fighters than you have."

"That," said Foreman, "may be a factor for me. I got a dog who fights all the time. He comes home whipped."

"Do you expect Ali to go for the eye?"

Foreman shrugged. "It's good for anybody to go for anything they can as long as they can. The crow will go for the scarecrow but run away from dynamic people."

"We hear you're writing a book."

"Oh," Foreman said in his mildest voice, "I just like to keep an account of what's going on."

"Do you have a subject for the book?"

"It'll be about me in general."

"Plan to publish it?"

He was thoughtful, as if contemplating the uncharted lands of literature that lay ahead. "I don't know," he said, "it may be just for my kids."

Reporter: "Do Ali's remarks bother you?"

Foreman: "No. He makes me think of a parrot who keeps saying, 'You're stupid, you're stupid.' Not to offend Muhammad Ali, but he's like that parrot. What he says, he's said before."

They asked him if he liked the country of Zaïre and he looked uneasy and said, first hint of uneasiness to his voice, "I would like to stay as long as possible and visit." If boxers were good liars, maybe he was no boxer.

"Why are you staying at the Inter-Continental instead of here?" Foreman replied even faster, "Well, I'm accustomed to hotel life. Although I like this place in Nsele." He was rescued by another query. "We hear President Mobutu gave you a pet lion."

Foreman brought back his smile. "He's big enough not to be a pet. He's a serious lion."

"Do you enjoy being Champ?" It was as if reporters had the license to ask any stupid question, any whatever. The trouble was that every reason existed for stupid questions. That was when the subject might reveal himself most. "You enjoy being Champ?"

"I think about it every night," said George, and added with a rush of compressed love for himself that he could not quite throttle into that soft voice, "I think about it and I thank God, and I thank George Foreman for having *true* endurance." The inevitable schizophrenia of great athletes was in his voice. Like artists, it is hard for them not to see the finished professional as a separate creature from the child that created him. The child (now grown up) still accompanies the great athlete and is wholly in love with him, an immature love, be it said.

But Sadler, Moore and Saddler had been teaching him to recover from mistakes. So his voice was quiet again and he added quickly, "I don't think I'm superior to any previous Champion. It's something I've borrowed, and I'll have to give it up." He turned expansive. "I even love to see young cats looking at me and saying, 'Aaah, I can take him,' and I laugh. I used to be that way. It's all right. That's how it ought to be." He looked so happy with this press conference that he had become a natural force in the room, and everyone liked him. He was a contrast to Ali who, when reporters were about, was always intent over the latest injury to his status and therefore rattled on the being of the media like a tin roof banging in the wind.

The questions continued. Foreman's answers came back with the velvet touch of a well-worn pair of dungarees. Only once did he give a clue to what he might be like in a temper. A reporter asked what he thought of Ali's claim that he was more militant in working for his people than Foreman.

George got stiff. The warp and woof were jamming the thread. His breath was a hint constricted. "There is no suggestion," he said, "that can bother someone who is intelligent. In answer to Ali being more militant . . ." But his voice rose. "I don't even think about things like that," he answered, cutting off the question. It was obvious that anger was upset in him as easily as tears from a spoiled child. There must be a massive instability to his faculties of rage, explanation in part for his rituals of concentration. Like the man who fears falling from high places, and fixes his eyes on the floor so that he need never look out a window, Foreman fixed his mind on the absence of disturbance.

"It's hard," said Foreman, "to concentrate and be polite when you're asked questions you've heard before." He subscribed to the principle that repetition kills the soul. "You see, I'm preparing for a fight. That's my interest. I don't want distraction. I have no quarrel with the press, but I like to keep my mind working on the things I set for it. You see," he said, "you have to be one hundred percent stable in everything you do." And he looked about him as if to indicate he had been talking long enough.

"George, one last question. What's your fight prediction?"

Foreman was home. It was over. "Oh," he said, in no faint parody, "I'm the greatest fighter who ever lived. I'm a wonder. The fifth wonder of the world. I'm even faster than Muhammad Ali. And I'm going to knock him out in three . . . two . . . one." He let his eyes laugh. "I'll be doing one hundred percent my best," he said. "That's my only prediction."

Now, Dick Sadler was asked a few questions. Short, stocky, about sixty, with a bald head, a flattened nose and a flat black beret sitting on his bald head, Foreman's manager was rough yet roly-poly, and formidable in his features for they were a map with renovations — Sadler knew how flesh got bent in the real world. Since he was also an amalgam of all that sly wisdom of manner that comes through the cross-fertilization of the various Black establishments: prison, boxing, music, even personal oratory, Sadler, if he had been an actor, could have played anything from a trusty on a chain gang to an aging emcee. He could have done a hoofer or a stand-up comedian, and had; could play piano or trumpet, and had. He was versatile and knew it by the age of nine, when he acted in "Our Gang" comedies. Even now his features made you think of such classic faces as Louis Armstrong or Moms Mabley; Sadler's mouth was always looking to digest the taste on his lips of the last remark. It was often original for he never needed to say the same thing twice. All the same he made a point of saying the same thing if talking to the press: "Repetition is security for idiots," said his sardonic look, and he developed his speeches. "George," he now told them, "is going to keep his left foot between Muhammad's legs. Oooh!" said Sadler in pain. "That's where George should be. Hit you in the kidney, hit you in the heart, hit you in the kidney again. Oooh! George does more things than Muhammad. Punches better, better all around, he's fast and more complete. George can slip, George can parry, George is going to catch you inside, spin you, hit you on the side of your head. You'll know and maybe you won't know." Sadler stopped, looked down, let himself wobble like a drunken man. "Your legs will know it."

Asked if there might be last-minute shifts in Foreman's training or strategy, Sadler shrugged at the flatness of the question. "I've been doing this for a gang of years with a gang of Champs. We're not worried. We don't have to dip into my *intuition* at the last instant. Ali can run but he sure

59

can't run for long. We're confident. There'll be no surprises. This ought to be the easiest fight George is going to have." He nodded to the press and took off with his fighter. "Gangway for all this talent," he cried out.

Something of this was clear in the way he had Foreman work next day. There was no boxing, and no fancy sparring, just the eerie sounds of Foreman's nature music ("I Love the Lord" — Donny Hathaway) and after fifteen or twenty minutes of loosening, brooding and shadowboxing, Foreman went to work on the heavy bag. Sadler stood holding it, a rudimentary exercise usually given to beginners who first must learn to punch into a stationary object. But Foreman and Sadler were practicing something else.

It is punishing for a boxer to have a long workout on a heavy bag. It hurts one's arms, it hurts one's head, it can spring one's knuckles if the hands are not wrapped. Big as a tackling dummy, the bag weighs eighty pounds or more, and when a punch is not thrown properly, the boxer's body shudders with the shock. It is like being brought down by an unexpected tackle. One bad punch is enough. Now Foreman began to hit this bag with lefts and rights. He did not throw them slowly, he did not throw them fast, he threw them steadily, putting all of his body into each punch, which came to mean that he was contracting and expelling his force forty to fifty times a minute for he threw that many punches, not fast, not slow, but concussive in their power. Sadler leaned forward, braced to the back of the bag, like a man riding a barrel in a storm at sea. He was shaken with every punch. His body quivered from the impact. That hardly mattered, that was part of the show.

When the impact of Foreman's fist on the other side of the bag was particularly heavy, he grunted, and said "Alors" in admiration.

Fifty punches a minute for a three-minute round. It is one hundred and fifty punches without rest. Foreman stopped hitting the bag for the thirty-second interval Sadler allowed between each round, but Foreman did not stop moving. The bag free, he danced about it, tapping it lightly, moving his feet faster and faster, and the thirty seconds up, Sadler was back holding the bag, and Foreman was pounding punches into it. These were no ordinary swings. Foreman was working for the maximum of power in punch after punch round after round fifty or a hundred punches in a row without diminishing his power — he would throw five or six hundred punches in this session, and they were probably the heaviest cumulative series of punches any boxing writer had seen. Each of these blows was enough to smash an average athlete's ribs; anybody with poor stomach muscles would have a broken spine. Foreman hit the heavy bag with the confidence of a man who can pick up a sledgehammer and knock down a tree. The bag developed a hollow as deep as his head. As the rounds went by, Foreman's sweat formed a pattern of drops six feet in diameter on the floor: poom! and pom! and boom! . . . bom! . . . boom! . . . went the sounds of his fists into the bag, methodical, rhythmic, and just as predictably hypnotic as the great overhead blow of the steam hammer driving a channel of steel into clay. One could feel the strategy. Sooner or later, there must come a time in the fight when Ali would be so tired he could not move, could only use his arms to protect himself. Then he would be like a heavy bag. Then Foreman would treat him like a heavy bag. In the immense and massive confidence of these enormous reverberating blows his fists would blast through every protection of Ali, smashing at those forearms until they could protect Ali no more. Six hundred blows at the heavy bag; not one false punch. His hands would be ready to beat on every angle of Ali's cowering and self-protective meat, and Sadler, as if reading the psychic temperature of comprehension in the audience, cried out from his wise gargoyle of a mouth, "Don't stand and freeze, Muhammad. Oh, Muhammad, don't you stand and freeze!"

5. DEAD MAN ON THE FLOOR

ALI WAS peeping in. There was not much Foreman could try that Ali did not see. The first to train each day in this same ring, Ali had all the time he needed to begin his workout at noon, talk to the press, walk the hundred yards back to his villa for a shower, and then come out again to take a squint at George. Foreman would arrive about 1 P.M. after a forty-mile drive from the Inter-Continental and go to a dressing room to change. Often he would arrive while Ali was still talking to the press. Hearing the sounds of Foreman's retinue passing outside Ali would shout, "Come on in, chump. I ain't going to hurt you."

Foreman would call back, "Don't want to hear that."

He would pass out of range of Ali's voice, and Ali would declare to the reporters listening, "George Foreman wants to keep his mind undisturbed because he's got a lot to worry about. He has to face *me*."

These days Ali seemed more interested in talking to the press than in working. One morning he did no more than three rounds of light shadowboxing. Then he hit the heavy bag for a few minutes. Maybe Ali had been hitting heavy bags for too many years, but he did it gingerly as if he did not wish to jar either his hands or his head. He seemed to be saving his energies for the press. He was always ready for a harangue after a workout, and there was something unchanging in his voice — the same hysteria one first heard ten years ago was still present — the jeering agitated voice that always repelled his white listeners, the ugly voice so much at odds with his customary charm. You could feel Ali shift the gears of his psyche as he went into it, as though it were a special transmission to use only for press conferences, or declaiming his poetry, or talking about his present opponent. At such times his tone would turn harsh. High-pitched hints of fear would come into his voice and large gouts of indignation. Even as what he said became more comical, so he would become more humorless. "Great as I am," he would state, "you have made me the underdog. I, an artist, a creator, am called the underdog when fighting an amateur." He would be kingly in disdain but it was probably for the castle of Camp since he knew that everything he said was put immediately into quotation marks. Something in his voice promised that you would never know how much he believed of what he had to say. After a while one could begin to suspect these speeches served as an organ of elimination to vent the boredom of training; he was sending his psychic wastes directly into the press. On the consequence, he was not exactly fun to be around. If he poisoned the air with his harangues, he raised the thought that he was in a continuing panic. He certainly had to be in some fear after those quick looks at

Foreman on the heavy bag. Some part of his gut had to respond to those monumental thuds. As if in reaction, he would assemble the press for still one more tirade. The voice of the tirade was, however, growing hollow, and there were occasions at Nsele when the hollow seemed to reverberate back, as if he sent out a call, "Hear, O walls, the sound of my greatness," and the walls did not hear him.

Thursday, five days before the bout, Ali gave a typical seminar. "This fight is going to be not only the largest boxing *eee*-vent, but it will prove to be the largest *eee*-vent in the history of the world. It will be the greatest upset of which anyone has ever heard, and to those who are ignorant of boxing, it will seem like the greatest miracle. The boxing public are fools and illiterates to the knowledge and art of boxing. This is because you here who write about boxing are ignorant of what you try to describe. You writers are the real fools and illiterates. I am going to demonstrate — so you will have something new for your columns — why I cannot be defeated by George Foreman and will create the greatest upset in the history of boxing which you by your ignorance and foolishness as writers have actually created. It is your fault," he said, mouthing his words for absolute enunciation, "that the boxing public knows so little and therefore believes George Foreman is great and I am finished. I must therefore demonstrate to you by scientific evidence how wrong you are. Angelo," he said to Angelo Dundee, "hand me those records, will you," and he began to read a list of fighters he had fought. The history of Heavyweight boxing in the last thirteen years was evoked by the list. His first seven fights were with pugilists never well

65

known, names like Herb Siler, Tony Esperti and Donnie Freeman. "Nobodies," said Ali in comment. By his eighth fight, he was in with Alonzo Johnson, "a ranked contender," then Alex Miteff, "a ranked contender," Willi Besmanoff, "a ranked contender." Now Ali made a sour face. "At a time when George Foreman was having his first street fights, I was already fighting ranked contenders, boxers of skill, sluggers of repute, dangerous men! Look at the list: Sonny Banks, Billy Daniels, Alejandro Lavorante, Archie Moore! Doug Jones, Henry Cooper, Sonny Liston! I fought them all. Patterson, Chuvalo, Cooper again, Mildenberger, Cleveland Williams — a dangerous Heavyweight. Ernie Terrell, twice the size of Foreman — I whupped him. Zora Folley — he saluted the American flag just like Foreman, and I knocked him out cold, a skilled boxer!" The ring apron at Nsele was six feet above the floor — thus another example of technology in Zaïre: a fighter falling through these ropes could fracture his skull on the drop to the floor — Ali sat on this apron, his legs dangling, and Bundini stood in front. It looked like Ali was sitting on his shoulders. So Bundini's head, rotund as a ball, close cropped and bald in the middle, rose in a protuberance between Ali's legs. While he spoke, Ali put his hands on Bundini's head as if a crystal ball (a black crystal ball!) were in his palms; each time he would pat Bundini's bald spot for emphasis, Bundini would glare at the reporters like a witch doctor in stocks. "To the press I say this," said Ali. "I fought twenty ranked contenders before Foreman had his first fight!" Ali sneered. How could the press in its ignorance begin to comprehend such boxing culture? "Now, let Angelo read the list of

Foreman's fights." As the names went by, Ali did not stop making faces. "Don Waldheim." "A nobody." "Fred Askew." "A nobody." "Sylvester Dullaire." "A nobody." "Chuck Wepner." "Nobody." "John Carroll." "Nobody." "Cookie Wallace." "Nobody." "Vernon Clay," said Dundee. Ali hesitated. "Vernon *Clay — he* might be good." The press laughed. They laughed again at Ali's comment for Gary "Hobo" Wiler — "a tramp." Now came a few more called "nobody." Ali said in disgust, "If I fought these bums, you people would put me out of the fight game." Abruptly Bundini shouted, "Next week, we be Champ again." "Shut up," said Ali, slapping him on the head, "it's my show."

When the full list of Foreman's fights had been delivered, Ali gave the summation. "Foreman fought a bum a month. In all, George Foreman fought five men with names. He stopped all five, but none took the count of ten. Of the twenty-nine name fighters I met, fifteen stayed down for the count of ten." With all the pride of having worked up a legal brief well organized and well delivered, Ali now addressed the jury. "I'm a boxing scholar. I'm a boxing scientist — this is scientific evidence. You ignore it at your peril if you forget that I am a dancing master, a great artist."

"Float like a butterfly, sting like a bee," shouted Bundini.

"Shut up," said Ali, slapping Bundini's bald spot. Then he looked hard at the press. "You are ignorant of boxing. You are ignorant men. You are impressed with George Foreman because he is so big and his muscles seem so big."

"They ain't," rumbled Bundini, "they ain't."

"Shut up," said Ali, rapping him.

"Now," said Ali, "I say to you in the press, you are impressed with Foreman because he looks like a big Black man and he hits a bag so hard. He cuts off the ring! I am going to tell you that he cannot fight. I will demonstrate that the night of the fight. You will see my ripping left and my shocking right cross. You are going to get the shock of your life. Because now you are impressed with Foreman. But I let you in on a secret. Colored folks scare more white folks than they scare colored folks. I am not afraid of Foreman, and that you will discover."

Next day, however, Ali varied the routine. There was no press conference. Instead, a drama took place in the ring. But then the fact that Ali was boxing today was in itself an event. In the last week and a half, he had sparred only three times, a light schedule. Of course, Ali had been training for so long his stablemates were growing old with him. Indeed, there was only one left, Roy Williams, the big dark gentle fighter who at Deer Lake had acted as if it were sacrilege to strike his employer. Now he was introduced by Bundini to the audience of several hundred Africans: "Ladies and gentlemen, this is Roy Williams, Heavyweight Champ of Pennsylvania. He's taller than George Foreman, he's heavier than George Foreman, his reach is longer, he hits harder, and he's more intelligent than George Foreman." Bundini was the father of hyperbole.

His remarks were translated by a Zairois interpreter to the Black audience. They giggled and applauded. Ali now led them in a chant, *"Ali boma yé, Ali boma yé,"* which translated as "Kill him, Ali" — an old fight cry when all is said — and Ali conducted his people through the chant, but strictly, laying firm strokes on the air, a choirmaster with a boy scout chorus, stern, not fooling, proud of his chickens, except a smile seemed to come off the act. Everybody was happy about it and the cry was without menace — nothing of cannibals savoring the meal to come or grunts and growls, more like a high school crowd crying "Slay Sisley High," a testimonial to Ali's good spirits. He looked eighteen this morning and he got ready to spar with Roy Williams.

They hardly boxed, however. After weeks and months of working together, a fighter and his sparring partner are an old married couple. They make comfortable love. That is all right for old married couples, but the dangers are obvious for a fighter. He gets used to living below the level of risk in the ring. So Ali dispensed today with all idea of boxing. He wrestled through an entire round with Williams. To the beat of Big Black on the floor beating on his conga drum, one sullen throbbing rhythm, Ali grappled up and down the ring. "I'm going to tie George up and walk with him, *walk* with him," Ali said in a loud throttled voice through his mouthpiece. "Yes, I'm going to walk with him." Occasionally, he would fall back to the ropes and let Williams pound him, then he would wrestle some more. "We're going to *walk* with him." When the round was over, Ali yelled to the side of the hall, "Archie Moore, number one spy, you tell George I'm running. I'm going to work him until he's stupid and then the torture begins. War! War!" Ali shouted, and rushed out swinging like an archetype of determination, only to go slack and wave to Williams to pound him on the ropes.

"Archie Moore, number one spy," he called over his shoulder even as Williams was hitting him.

Ali had fought Moore more than ten years ago. Not yet

Champion then, not even any world-soul larger than Cassius Clay, the Louisville Lip, he had still made predictions the fight would end in four. Archie came into the ring overweight and overage, but he nearly knocked The Lip out in the first round. He caught him a powerful sneak punch and as Cassius staggered back, Moore threw one of his best right hands. If it had hit, the fight might have been over, but Clay, half-unconscious, managed to avoid it. After that, the fight went to Cassius. By the end of the third round, Moore's legs were so used up he did not sit down on his stool. He remained standing in his corner for fear that once seated, he would not have the strength to get up and answer the bell. He did not, of course, last through the fourth, and it was the end of his career. Archie Moore, with a record of something like two hundred fights, once Light-Heavyweight Champion, and in the ring for the Heavyweight title twice, was retired by Cassius Clay: something of the echo of that night was in Ali's voice as he cried, "Number one spy!" as if, indeed, it still irritated Ali that he, the first disciple of Moore's art, should find the old master in his opponent's employ. Of course, there was no reason for Moore to love Ali, who had never acknowledged his artistic debt. For that matter, Archie had hardly been given full credit for how much he influenced other boxers. Once, in answer to the Irish fighter Roger Donoghue, who asked how Moore could throw punches out of a position that kept his arms crossed in front of his face, Archie replied, "You're talking about technique, Roger, and what I do is philosophy." Moore may indeed have brought boxing over to philosophy. He was probably the first to articulate (and he was strikingly articulate) that not all heavy punches were heavy, not all traps worth avoiding nor all openings there to be taken, not all exhaustions should be thought depleting, nor all ring ropes constricting to one's back, no corner had to be without room to fight, no knockdown was like any other, and no paradox could ever press upon you without offering its compressed power. Moore was to boxing what Nimzovitch had been to chess. (Ali, needless to say, could offer his considerable parallel to Bobby Fischer when it came to heckling an opponent out of his skin.)

These days Moore looked like an orotund Black professor who played a saxophone on weekends. His gray mustache curved down on each side of his mouth in a benign Fu Manchu, and his sideburns grew like mutton chops — a plump and dashing man in late middle age. What a titillation to recognize that he was close to sixty and yet had been in the ring with Ali.

Moore's presence as the first philosopher of boxing must have been encouraging Ali to reveal himself as pugilism's master of the occult. He proceeded to get himself knocked out by his sparring partner. A ritual knockout.

As the second round began, Ali beckoned for Williams to belabor his belly. Obediently, Williams came forward and pounded at Ali's capacity to absorb endless punches to the stomach. "Oooh, it hurts," Ali yelled suddenly. "It huuuuurts!"

Quickly the Zairois interpreter said to the Blacks in the back seats: "*Il frappe dur.*" Ali came off the ropes and wrestled again with Williams. As they walked, Ali made a speech to Moore. "Your man has no class," he cried loud

71

and clear through his rubber mouthpiece, "no footwork. He thinks slow. The turkey is ready for the killing." Moore smiled benignly as though to reply, "Not saying which turkey."

Ali went back to the ropes. Williams hit him in the stomach. Ali sank to one knee. A trainer, Walter Youngblood, jumped into the ring and counted to eight. Ali got up and staggered about. He and Williams now looked equal to two sumo wrestlers with sand in their eyes. "He goin' for my gut," grunted Ali in a sad plantation voice and on the next punch to the stomach went down again. "The man been knocked down twice," cried Ali, and leaped to his feet. Sparring continued. So did more knockdowns. Each was occasion for a speech. After the fourth — or was it the fifth? — knockdown Ali stayed down. To everybody's surprise, Walter Youngblood counted to ten. The mood was awful. It was as if somebody had told an absolutely filthy joke that absolutely didn't work. A devil's fart. The air was ruined. From the floor, Ali said: "Well, The Lip has been shut. He's had his mouth shut for the last time. George Foreman is the greatest. Too strong," said Ali sadly. "He hit too hard. Now, a defeated Ali leaves the ring. George Foreman is undisputed champion of the world."

The Africans in the rear of the hall were stricken. A silence, not without dread, was rising from them. Nobody believed Ali had been hurt — they were afraid of something worse. By way of this charade, Ali had given a tilt to the field of forces surrounding the fight. As a dead man had he spoken from the floor. Like a member of a chorus had he offered the comment: "He's had his mouth shut for the last time." The African audience reacted uneasily, as if his words could excite unseen forces. There was hardly a Zairois in the audience who did not know that Mobutu, good president, was not only a dictator but a doctor of the occult with a pygmy for his own private conjuror, (distinguished must that pygmy be!). If, however, Mobutu had his *féticheur,* who among these Africans would not believe Ali was also a powerful voice in the fearful and magical zone between the living and the dead. The hush which fell on the crowd (like the silence in a forest after the echo of a rifle) was at the unmitigated horror of what Ali might be doing if he did not know what he had done. A man should not offer his limbs to sorcery any more than he might encourage his soul to slip into the mists. When every word reverberates to the end of the earth, a weak word can bring back an echo to punish the man who spoke; a weak action guarantee defeat. Therefore, a man must not play with his dignity unless he is adept in the arts of transformation. Did Ali really know what he was doing? Was he foolishly trying to burn away some taint in his soul and thereby daring disaster, or was he purposefully arousing the forces working for the victory of Foreman in order to disturb them? Who could know?

Ali now leaped to his feet and reassured the crowd. "Tell them," he said to the interpreter, "that this is only a treat. The people will not see it ever in real life. Tell the people to cheer up. No man is strong enough or great enough to knock me out. *Ali boma yé,*" he said. "Tell them to *boma yé.*" The translation came. Wan cheers. The shock would demand its time for recovery. The Africans were numb. Do not try to think until thought returns, their mood may have said. Nonetheless, they cried out *"Boma yé."* Who had ever heard such confidence as one heard from the man in the ring? The laws of highest magic might be in his employ.

"Jive suckers," said Ali crooning to the press, "hear what I say. When you see me rapping like this, please don't bet against me."

Big Black tapped the conga drum, and Foreman passed at this moment on the walk outside. "There's a war going on," cried Ali, and so speaking, got out of the ring and moved off to his quarters. One had time to recall Ali's dream announced those many weeks ago when he first arrived in Zaïre. He had said then that Foreman's eye would be cut. Bundini had boasted that he was working the magic to make a cut. Then Foreman was cut. But a week too soon. If Ali and Bundini had been employing powers, their powers proved misapplied. Were they now being laid on closer? Much to think about in the week of this fight.

6. OUR BLACK KISSINGER

N'GOLO WAS a Congolese word for force, for vital force. Equally could it be applied to ego, status, strength or libido. Indubitably did Ali feel deprived of his rightful share. For ten years, the press had been cheating Ali of n'golo. No matter if he had as much as anyone in America, he wanted more. It is not the n'golo you have, but the n'golo you are denied that excites the harshest hysterias of the soul. So he could not want to lose this fight. If he did, they would write up the epitaphs for his career, and the dead have no n'golo. The dead are dying of thirst — so goes an old African saying. The dead cannot dwell in the n'golo that arrives with the first swallow of palm wine, whisky, or beer.

Ali's relations with the press were now nonstop. Never did a fighter seem to have so much respect for the magical power of the written word. His villa with the High Schlock furniture was open to many a reporter, and in the afternoons at Nsele after training was over for both men, Foreman would ride back to the Inter-Continental and Ali would lie about in his living room, legs extended from a low armchair, his valuable arms folded on his chest, and answer more questions from the reporters sitting with him, his iron endurance for conversation never in question. He ran a marathon every day with his tongue, strong, sure and never stumbling over anyone else's thought. If a question were asked for which he had no reply, he would not hear it. Majestic was the snobbery of his ear.

He was, of course, friendly to Black correspondents — indeed, interviewing Muhammad was often their apprenticeship. With no other famous Black man were they likely to receive as much courtesy: Ali answered questions in full. He answered them to microphones for future radio programs and to microphones for reporters with tape recorders, he slowed up his speech for journalists taking notes, and was relaxed if one did not take a note. He was weaving a mighty bag of burlap large enough to cover the earth. When it was finished he would put the world in that bag and tote it on his shoulder.

So in the easy hours of the afternoon that followed his knockout in training by Roy Williams he returned to his favorite scenario and described in detail how he would vanquish Foreman. "Just another gym workout," he said. "The fight will be easy. This man does not want to take a head whipping like Frazier just to beat you. He's not as tough as Frazier. He's soft and spoiled."

A young Black named Sam Clark working for BAN (Black Audio Network), which offered Black news to Black-oriented stations, now asked a good question. "If you were to advise Foreman how to fight you, what would you tell him?"

"If I," said Ali, "give the enemy some of my knowledge, then maybe he'll have sense to lay back and wait. Of course I will even convert that to my advantage. I'm versatile. All the same, the Mummy's best bet is to stand in the center of the ring and wait for me to come in." With hardly a pause, he added, "Did you hear that *death* music he plays? He *is* a mummy. And," said Ali chuckling, "I'm going to be the Mummy's Curse!"

Topics went by. He spoke of Africans learning the technology of the world. "Usually you feel safer if you see a white face flying a plane," he said. "It just seems like a white man should fix the jet engine. Yet here they are all Black. That impressed me very much," he said. Of course when he was most sincere, so could he mean it least. In a similar conversation with friends, he had winked and added, "I never believe the bullshit that the pilots is all Black. I keep looking for the secret closet where they hide the white man until the trouble starts." He winked, as if this remark need have no more validity than the previous one.

"Are you going to try to hit Foreman's cut?" asked another Black reporter.

"I'm going to hit *around* the cut," answered Ali. "I'm going to beat him good," he said out of the bottomless funds of his indignation, "and I want the credit for winning. I don't want to give it to the cut." He made a point of saying, "After I win, they talk about me fighting for ten million dollars."

"If they do, will you still retire?"

"I don't know. I'm going home with no more than one million, three hundred thousand. Half of the five million

77

goes to the Government, then half a million for expenses and one-third to my manager. I'm left with one million three. That ain't no money. You give me a hundred million today, I'll be broke tomorrow. We got a hospital we're working on, a Black hospital being built in Chicago, costs fifty million dollars. My money goes into causes. If I win this fight, I'll be traveling everywhere." Now the separate conversations had come together into one and he talked with the same muscular love of rhetoric that a politician has when he is giving his campaign speech and knows it is a good one. So Ali was at last in full oration. "If I win," said Ali, "I'm going to be the Black Kissinger. It's full of glory, but it's tiresome. Every time I visit a place, I got to go by the schools, by the old folks' home. I'm not just a fighter, I'm a world figure to these people" — it was as if he had to keep saying it the way Foreman had to hit a heavy bag, as if the sinews of his will would steel by the force of this oral conditioning. The question was forever growing. Was he still a kid from Louisville talking, talking, through the afternoon, and for all anyone knew through the night, talking through the ungovernable anxiety of a youth seized by history to enter the dynamos of history? Or was he in full process of becoming that most unique phenomenon, a twentieth century prophet, and so the anger and the fear of his voice was that he could not teach, could not convince, could not convince? Had any of the reporters made a face when he spoke of himself as the Black Kissinger? Now, as if to forestall derision, he clowned. "When you visit all these folks in all these strange lands, you got to eat. That's not so easy. In America they offer you a drink. A fighter can turn down a drink. Here, you got to eat. They're hurt if you don't eat. It's an honor to be loved by so many people, but it's hell, man."

He could not, however, stay away from his mission. "Nobody is ready to know what I'm up to," he said. "People in America just find it hard to take a fighter seriously. They don't know that I'm using boxing for the sake of getting over certain points you couldn't get over without it. Being a fighter enables me to attain certain ends. I'm not doing this," he muttered at last, "for the glory of fighting, but to change a lot of things."

It was clear what he was saying. One had only to open to the possibility that Ali had a large mind rather than a repetitive mind and was ready for oncoming chaos, ready for the volcanic disruptions that would boil through the world in these approaching years of pollution, malfunction and economic disaster. Who knew what camps the world would yet see? Here was this tall pale Negro from Louisville, born to be some modern species of flunky to some bourbon-minted redolent white voice, and instead was living with a vision of himself as a world leader, president not of America, or even of a United Africa, but leader of half the Western world, leader doubtless of future Black and Arab republics. Had Muhammad Mobutu Napoleon Ali come for an instant face to face with the differences between Islam and Bantu?

On the shock of this recognition, that Ali's seriousness might as well be rooted in the molten iron of the earth, and his craziness not necessarily so crazy, Norman came near for a word. "I know what you're saying," he said to Muhammad.

"I'm serious," said Ali.

"Yes, I know you are." He thought of Foreman's Herculean training and Ali's contempt. "You better win this fight," he heard himself stating, "because if you don't, you are going to be a professor who gives lectures, that's all."

"I'm going to win."

"You might have to work like you never did before. Foreman has become a sophisticated fighter."

"Yes," said Ali, in a quiet voice, one line for one interviewer at last, "yes," said Ali, "I know that." He added with a wry small touch, "George is much improved."

Talk went on. Endless people came and went. Ali ate while photographers photographed his open mouth. Not since Louis XV sat on his *chaise-percée* and delivered the royal stool to the royal pot to be instantly carried away by the royal chamberlain had a man been so observed. No other politician or leader of the world would leave himself so open to scrutiny. What a limitless curiosity could Ali generate.

On the strength of his own curiosity about the qualities of Ali's condition, Norman asked if he could run with him tonight. Inquiring, he learned that Ali would be going to bed at nine and setting the alarm for three. Norman would have to be back at the villa then.

"You can't keep up with me," said Ali.

"I don't intend to try. I just want to run a little."

"Show up," said Ali with a shrug.

HE COULD GO back to the Inter-Continental, eat early and try to get some sleep before the run, but sleep was not likely between eight in the evening and midnight — besides there was no question of keeping up with Muhammad. His conscience, however (now on the side of good journalism), was telling him that the better his own condition, the more he would be able to discern about Ali's. What a pity he had not been jogging since the summer. Up in Maine he had done two miles every other day, but jogging was one discipline he could not maintain. At five feet eight inches and one hundred and seventy pounds, Norman was simply too heavy to enjoy running. He could jog at a reasonable gait — fifteen minutes for two miles was good time for him — and if pushed, he could jog three miles, conceivably four, but he hated it. Jogging disturbed the character of one's day. He did not feel refreshed afterward but overstimulated and irritable. The truth of jogging was it only felt good when you stopped. And he would remind himself that with the exception of Erich Segal and

George Gilder, he had never heard of a writer who liked to run — who wanted the brilliance of the mind discharged through the ankles?

Back in Kinshasa, he decided to have drinks and a good meal after all, and during dinner there was amusement at the thought he would accompany Ali on the road. "You know you have to do it," said John Vinocur of the AP. "I know," said Mailer, in full gloom. "Ali isn't expecting me to show up, but he won't forgive it if I don't." "That's right, that's right," said Vinocur, "I offered to run with Foreman once, and when I didn't get there, he never let me forget. He brings it up every time I see him."

"Plimpton, you've got to come with me," said Mailer.

George Plimpton wasn't sure he would. Mailer knew he wouldn't. Plimpton had too much to lose. With his tall thin track man's body and his quietly buried competitive passion (large as Vesuvius, if smokeless) Plimpton would have to keep on some kind of close terms with Ali or pay a disproportionate price in humiliation. Whereas it was easy for Mailer. If he didn't get a leg cramp in the first five hundred yards, he could pick the half-mile mark to take his bow. He just hoped Ali didn't run too fast. That would be jogger's hell. At the thought of being wiped out from the start, a little bile rose from the drinks and the rich food. It was now only nine in the evening, but his stomach felt as if the forces of digestion were in stupor.

Still, it was a good meal. They were eating in the open air with the funky grandeur of a dilapidated grand hotel for backdrop. The Palace Hotel. It was now an apartment house and offered its miasma — there was from time to time an operative whiff of what Victorians used to call *the smell of drains*. The toilet in the restroom was rimless, a needless even excrementitious detail if not for the fact that our man of wisdom was hoping to move himself properly before going out to run, but the sight of the bowl, the missing seat and the indescribable condition closed off his chances. Worse may have been glimpsed in many an American gas station, but never so settled in. SANICONGO was the brand name of the toilet, and it looked to have been installed in time for the coronation of King Leopold. Maybe the bowl even had its kuntu, for when he got back to the table, Horst Fass was telling stories about Vietnam, and they were in the mode of SANICONGO. Fass worked with Vinocur, and had the job — no casual responsibility — of making certain the communications of the AP would get out for the fight, a nightmare of telephones, teletypes, Telexes, Telstars and hysterical assistants. He was a cool and cheerful young German with all the confidence of his trades — not only a top technician but a reporter, a cameraman. He had been the AP man in many a war, many a port and many an international conference: not surprising that he also had a journalist's eye for the fine stories that cannot be used. So Mailer and Plimpton learned for the first time — be certain their mouths were open — that certain Americans in Nam had volunteered to be undertakers because they were connoisseurs of necrophilia and enjoyed making love to parts of a human body rather than the predictable dead whole. Fass told this with the expression of a man who has seen everything and so will never again be shocked but is nonetheless attached to the detail because it is an example of the extreme. As if this story, however, had been entree of wild boar, and one needed sherbet for dessert, Fass offered a touching tale about the brothels managed by the U.S. Army, a preventive measure against the special virulence of Vietnamese V.D.; there in the military brothels, the girls wore yellow and red badges, one color underwriting disease-free copulation and the other holding them in temporary chastity. Nonetheless, they could still work. At a lower rate. They were on hand for men who just wished to talk to a girl. "They did good business," said Fass. "A lot of the GIs just wanted to talk."

A little later, they all went to a Casino and played Black Jack. The thought that he would run with Ali was beginning to offer its agreeable tension, a sensation equal to the way he felt when he was going to win at Black Jack. Gambling had its own libido. Just as one was ill-advised to make love when libido was dim, so was that a way to lose money in gambling. Whenever he felt empty, he dropped his stake; when full of himself, he often won. Every gambler was familiar with the principle — it was visceral, after all — few failed to disobey it in one fashion or another. But never had he felt its application so powerfully as in Africa. It was almost as if one could make a living in Kinshasa provided one gambled only when one's blood was up.

Naturally, he drank a little. He had friends at this Casino. The manager was a young American not yet twenty-one and in love with the taste of his life in Africa; the croupiers and dealers were English girls, sharp as birds in their accents — the keen vibrating intelligence of the London working class was in their quick voices. He was getting *mal d'Afrique,* the sweet infection that forbids you to get out of Africa (in your mind, at least) once you have visited it. What intoxication to gamble and know in advance whether one would win or lose. Even orange juice and vodka gave its good thump. He was loving everything about the evening but the sluggishness of his digestion. Pocketing his money, he went back to the hotel to put on a T-shirt and exercise pants.

The long drive to Nsele, forty-five minutes and more, confirmed him in the first flaw of his life. He was a monster of bad timing. Why had he not paced himself so that the glow he was feeling at the Casino would be with him when he ran? Now his n'golo was fading with the drinks. By the time they hit the road, he would have to work off the beginnings of a hangover. And his stomach, that invariably reliable organ, had this night simply not digested his food. My God. A thick fish chowder and a pepper steak were floating down the Congo of his inner universe like pads of hyacinth in the clotted Zaïre. My God, add ice cream, rum and tonic, vodka and orange juice. Still, he did not feel sick, just turgid — a normal state for his fifty-one years, his heavy meals, and this hour.

It was close to three in the morning as he reached Nsele, and he would have preferred to go to sleep. He was even ready to consider turning around without seeing Ali. By now, however, that was hardly a serious alternative.

But the villa was dark. Maybe Ali would not run tonight. A couple of soldiers, polite but somewhat confused by the sight of visitors at this hour — Bob Drew, a cameraman from the AP, was also waiting — asked them not to knock on the door. So they all sat in the dark for a quarter of an hour, and then a few lights went on in the villa, and Howard Bingham, a young Black from *Sports Illustrated* who had virtually become Ali's private photographer, came by and brought them in. Ali was still sleepy. He had gone to bed at nine and just awakened, the longest stretch of sleep he would take over twenty-four hours. Later, after running, he might nap again, but sleep never seemed as pervasive a concern to him as to other fighters.

"You did come," he said with surprise, and then seemed to pay no further attention. He was doing some stretching exercises to wake up and had the surliness of any infantryman awakened in the middle of the night. They would make four for the run. Bingham was coming along and Pat Patterson, Ali's personal bodyguard, a Chicago cop, no darker than Ali, with the solemn even stolid expression of a man who has gone through a number of doors in his life without the absolute certainty that he would walk out again. By day, he always carried a pistol; by night — what a pity not to remember if he strapped a holster over his running gear.

Ali looked sour. The expression on his face was not difficult to read. Who wanted to run? He gave an order to one of the two vans that would accompany them, telling it to be certain to stay well behind, so that its fumes would not bother them. The other had Bob Drew inside to take photographs, and it was allowed to stay even.

Norman may have hoped the fighter would want to walk for a while, but Ali right away took off at a slow jogger's gait, and the others fell in. They trotted across the grass of the villas set parallel to the river and, when they came to the end of the block, took a turn toward the highway two miles off and kept trotting at the same slow pace past smaller villas, a species of motel row where some of the press was housed. It was like running in the middle of the night across suburban lawns on some undistinguished back street of Beverly Hills, an occasional light still on in a room here and there, one's eyes straining to pick up the driveways one would have to cross, the curbings, and the places where little wire fences protected the plantings. Ali served as a guide, pointing to holes in the ground, sudden dips, and slippery spots where hoses had watered the grass too long. And they went on at the same slow steady pace. It was, in fact, surprisingly slow, certainly no faster than his own rate when jogging by himself, and Norman felt, everything considered, in fairly good condition. His stomach was already a full soul of heated lead, and it was not going to get better, but to his surprise, it was not getting worse — it seemed to have settled in as one of the firm discontents he would have on this run.

After they had gone perhaps half a mile, Ali said, "You're in pretty good shape, Norm."

"Not good enough to talk," he answered through closed teeth.

Jogging was an act of balance. You had to get to the point where your legs and your lungs worked together in some equal state of exertion. They could each be close to overexertion, but if one was not more fatigued than the other, they offered some searing and hardworking equivalent of the tireless, to wit, you would feel no more abominable after a mile than after the first half mile. The trick was to reach this disagreeable state without having to favor the legs or the lungs. Then, if no hills were there to squander one's small reserve, and one did not lose stride or have to stop, if one did not stumble and one did not speak, that steady progressive churning could continue, thoroughgoing, raw to one's middle-aged insides, but virtuous — one felt like the motors of an old freighter.

After a few weeks of steady running, one could take the engines of the old freighter through longer and longer storms, one could manage hills, one could even talk (and how well one could ski later in the year with the legs built up!) but now his body has been docked for two months and he was performing a new kind of balancing act. It was not only his legs and his lungs but the gauges on the bile in his stomach he had to watch, and the pressure on his heart. If he had always run before breakfast, and so was unaccustomed to jogging with food in his stomach, he was having an education in that phenomenon now. It was a third factor, hot, bilious, and working like a bellows in reverse, for it kept pushing up a pressure on his lungs, yet, to his surprise, not nauseating, just heavy pressure, so that he knew he could not keep up with a faster pace more than a little before his stomach would be engorging his heart and both pounding in his ears.

Still, they had covered what must be three-quarters of a mile by now and were long past the villas and formal arrangement of Nsele's buildings, and just padded along on a back road with the surprisingly disagreeable exhaust of the lead van choking their nostrils. What a surprising impediment to add to the run — it had to be worse than cigar smoke at ringside, and to this pollution of air came an intermittent freaking of a photographic flash pack from Bob Drew's camera.

Still, he had acquired his balance. What with food, drink, and lack of condition, it was one of the most unpleasant runs he had ever made, certainly the most caustic in its preview of hell, but he had found his balance. He kept on running with the others, the gait most happily not stepped up, and came to recognize after a while that Ali was not a bad guy to run with. He kept making encouraging comments, "Hey, you're doin' fine, Norm," and, a little later, "Say, you're in good condition," to which the physical specimen could only grunt for reply — mainly it was the continuing sense of a perfect pace to Ali's legs that helped the run, as if his own legs were somehow being tuned to pick their own best rate, yes, something easy and uncompetitive came off Ali's good stride.

"How old are you, Norm?"

He answered in two bursts, "Fifty — one."

"Say, when I'm fifty-one, I won't be strong enough to run to the corner," said Ali. "I'm feeling tired already."

They jogged. Wherever possible, Ali ran on the turf. Pat Patterson, used to pounding concrete, ran on the paving of the road, and Bingham alternated. Norman stayed on the turf. It was generally easier on the feet and harder on the lungs to jog over grass, and his lungs so close to the pressure of his stomach were more in need than his legs, but he could not keep the feel of Ali's easy rhythm if he left the turf.

On they went. Now they were passing through a small

forest, and by his measure, they had come a little more than a mile. He was beginning to think it was remotely possible that he could cover the entire distance — was it scheduled for three miles? — but even as he was contemplating the heroics of this horror they entered on a long slow grade uphill, and something in the added burden told him that he was not going to make it without a breakdown in the engines. His heart had now made him prisoner — it sat in an iron collar around his neck, and as they chugged up the long slow grade, the collar tightened every fifty feet. He was breathing now as noisily as he had ever breathed, and recognized that he was near to the end of his run.

"Champ," he said, "I'm going — to stop — pretty soon," a speech in three throttled bursts. "I'm just — holding you — back," and realized it was true — except how could Ali put up with too slow a gait when the fight was just four nights away? "Anyway — have good run," he said, like the man in the water waving in martyred serenity at the companions to whom he has just offered his spot in the lifeboat. "I'll see you — back there."

And he returned alone. Later, when he measured it by the indicator on his car, he found that he had run with them for a mile and a half, not too unrespectable. And enjoyed his walk. Actually, he was a little surprised at how slow the pace had been. It seemed unfitting that he had been able to keep up as long as he had. If Ali were going to run for fifteen rounds, there should, he thought, be something more kin to a restlessness in his legs tonight. Of course, Ali was not wearing sneakers but heavy working shoes. Still. The leisureliness of the pace made him uneasy.

There is no need to follow Norman back on his walk, except that we are about to discover a secret to the motivation of writers who achieve a bit of prominence in their own time. As the road continued through the forest, dark as Africa is ever supposed to be, he was enjoying for the first time a sense of what it meant to be out alone in the African night, and occasionally, when the forest thinned, knew what it might also mean to be alone under an African sky. The clarity of the stars! The size of the bowl of heaven! Truth, thoughts after running are dependably banal. Yet what a teeming of cricket life and locusts in the brush about him, that nervous endless vibration seeming to shake the earth. It was one of the final questions: Were insects a part of the cosmos or the termites of the cosmos?

Just then, he heard a lion roar. It was no small sound, more like thunder, and it opened an unfolding wave of wrath across the sky and through the fields. Did the sound originate a mile away, or less? He had come out of the forest, but the lights of Nsele were also close to a mile away, and there was all of this deserted road between. He could never reach those lights before the lion would run him down. Then his next thought was that the lion, if it chose, could certainly race up on him silently, might even be on his way now.

Once, sailing in Provincetown harbor on nothing larger than a Sailfish, he had passed a whale. Or rather the whale passed him. A frolicsome whale which cavorted in its passage and was later to charm half the terrified boats in its path. He had recognized at the moment that there was nothing he could ever do if the whale chose to swallow him with his boat. Yet he felt singularly cool. What a perfect way to go. His place in American literature would be forever secure. They would seat him at Melville's feet. Melville and Mailer, ah, the consanguinity of the M's and the L's — how critics would love Mailer's now discovered preoccupations (see Croft on the mountain in *The Naked and the Dead*) with Ahab's Moby Dick.

Something of this tonic sangfroid was with him now. To be eaten by a lion on the banks of the Congo — who could fail to notice that it was Hemingway's own lion waiting down these years for the flesh of Ernest until an appropriate substitute had at last arrived?

They laughed back at Ali's villa when he told them about the roar. He had forgotten Nsele had a zoo and lions might as well be in it.

Ali looked tired. He had run another mile and a half, he would estimate, three miles in all, and had sprinted uphill for the last part, throwing punches, running backward, then all-out forward again, and was very tired now. "That running," he said, "takes more out of me than anything I ever felt in the ring. It's even worse than the fifteenth round, and that's as bad as you can get."

Like an overheated animal, Ali was lying on the steps of his villa, cooling his body against the stone, and Bingham, Patterson and Ali did not talk too much for a while. It was only 4 A.M. but the horizon was beginning to lighten — the dawn seemed to come in for hours across the African sky. Predictably, Ali was the one to pick up conversation again. His voice was surprisingly hoarse: he sounded as if a cold were coming on. That was all Ali needed — a chest cold for the fight! Pat Patterson, hovering over him like a truculent nurse, brought a bottle of orange juice and scolded him for lying on the stone, but Ali did not move. He was feeling sad from the rigors of the workout and talked of Jurgin Blin and Blue Lewis and Rudi Lubbers. "Nobody ever heard of them," he said, "until they fought me. But they trained to fight me and fought their best fights. They were good fighters against me," he said almost with wonder. (Wonder was as close as he ever came to doubt.) "Look at Bugner — his greatest fight was against me. Of course, I didn't train for any of them the way they trained for me. I couldn't. If I trained for every fight the way I did for this, I'd be dead. I'm glad I left myself a little bit for this one." He shook his head in a blank sort of self-pity as if some joy that once resided in his juices had been expended forever. "I'm going to get one million three hundred thousand for this fight, but I would give one million of that up gladly if I could just buy my present condition without the work."

Yet his present condition was so full of exhaustion. As if anxiety about the fight stirred in the hour before dawn, a litany began. It was the same speech he had made a day and a half ago to the press, the speech in which he listed each of Foreman's opponents and counted the number who were nobodies and the inability of Foreman to knock his opponents out cold. Patterson and Bingham nodded in the sad patience of men who worked for him and loved him and put up with this phase of his conditioning while Ali gave the speech the way a patient with a threatening heart will take a nitroglycerin pill. And Norman, with his food still undigested and his bowels hard packed from the shock

93

of the jogging, was blank himself when he tried to think of amusing conversation to divert Ali's mood. It proved up to Ali to change the tone and by the dawn he did. After showering and dressing he showed a magic trick and then another, long cylinders popping out of his hands to become handkerchiefs, and, indeed, next day at training, still haranguing the press, Ali ended by saying, "Foreman will never catch me. When I meet George Foreman, I'll be free as a bird," and he held up his hand and opened it. A bird flew out. To the vast delight of the press. Ali was writing the last line of their daily piece from Kinshasa today. Nor did it take them long to discover the source. Bundini had captured the bird earlier in the day and slipped it to Ali when the time came. Invaluable Bundini, improvisatory Bundini.

Still, as Norman drove home to the Inter-Continental and breakfast, he measured Ali's run. He had finished by the Chinese pagoda. That was two and a half miles, not three! Ali had run very slowly for the first mile and a half. With an empty stomach and the fair condition of the summer in Maine, he thought he could probably have kept up with Ali until the sprint at the end. It was no way for a man fighting for a Heavyweight title to do roadwork. Norman did not see how Ali could win. Defeat was in the air Ali alone seemed to refuse to breathe.

8. ELMO IN ZAÏRE

NEXT DAY, while watching Foreman at Ping-Pong, he had cause to wonder whether he was too pessimistic. The Heavyweight Champion of the World had been playing every day, but he was no phenomenon. He held his racket in a penholder grip and it was awkward to his purposes; he did not have a driving game, and the penholder is best for its facility in backhand slams. Foreman was certainly not experienced enough to put up more than a steady defense against Archie Moore, and that was hardly enough. Moore invariably won. Old competitive Archie, never an athlete to overlook an advantage, brought his special paddle to the fray, and it was as thick in foam rubber as the rear seat of a Cadillac. The sauciest tongue in London could not have given more English to the ball. A professional game hunter once remarked that the most dangerous animal he ever faced in Africa was a charging leopard. He thought his eyes were playing tricks for the cat moved like jump cuts in a movie film. That was how Archie's serve worked. He did not have much of a game beyond that, just lots of foam rubber, but he hardly needed more. The serve was formidably cockeyed. He would invariably beat George.

Foreman was good-natured about it. Dressed in one of his twenty sets of bib overalls, his biceps gleamed with his sweat, and his face grinned with the happy if unsuccessful effort to keep up with Archie's bouncing ball. When he would miss, and try to catch the ball on the ground before it reached the pool, the Champion would look like a big dog putting an uncertain paw on a mouse, somewhat bemused by the trickiness of it all. The thought occurred that Ali would play Ping-Pong better. With his intricate quickness of hand and eye, how could he not?

Every fighter had a part of the body you remembered. With Joe Frazier, it was the legs. They were not even like tree trunks, more like truncated gorillas pushing forward, working uphill, pushing forward. Foreman had something like Samson's arms — he could pull down the pillars of the temple. And Ali? He had a face, and arms to punish anyone who came near that face. He had fast feet. He would play Ping-Pong better. His wrists would be ready for every trick of Archie. Each unexpected bounce would speed his reflex. Whereas Foreman would find zephyrs, feathers and Ping-Pong balls alien to him.

Of course, George's strength would not be here. His leverage came from confrontation. The air of Foreman's camp was that George could afford to be seen playing games at which he was not adept. Let the world see his lack of lightning reflexes at the Ping-Pong table. It did not matter. The fight was a conclusion that could not be altered. If Ali entered the ring with fear, there would be a scandalously quick end. If Ali came in bravely, well, said the mood that came off everyone near Foreman, it would then be a more interesting fight, and Ali could even win a round or two, reflex would steal its points from confrontation, but it could not go on. Ali did not have the stamina to go fifteen rounds at top speed. As Foreman's people saw it, Ali's chances depended on speed, then more speed, then startling spurts of speed. Everybody repeated Henry Clark's remark, "One round with Foreman is like ten with another fighter." Yes, it would be equal to avoiding a keyed-up lion in a cage — not for one minute but for forty-five minutes.

Toward the end of his career, Archie Moore used to go fifteen rounds when he was hardly in condition to walk a mile. He had acquired the skill to avoid a murderous punch by a languid tilt of his chin. Why rush to move six inches when half an inch would provide? So Moore knew how long a trip you could get out of the oldest body. Leisure in the ring and absolute cool, no unnecessary movements, feel no fear and show a few tricks — that was the last substitute for condition. It would work until pressure was on. No one knew better than Moore. Ali had exposed him over the four rounds of their fight because Ali kept the pressure on. Now, in his turn, Foreman would eat up the best of Ali's condition, consume his stamina, use up his surprises. Then it would be Ali on the ropes and Foreman working on the heavy bag.

"Sadler, Moore, and Saddler," wrote Archie Moore for *Sports Illustrated*, "are devising new approaches to force; to coerce, fool and browbeat the sensitive Ali into a close confrontation with Foreman, who not only has TNT in his mitts but *nuclearology* as well. . . ." That was the confidence in Foreman's camp at the Inter-Continental, he had nuclearology in his fists. The scene at the Ping-Pong table and the pool, the scene under every umbrella and before every sunbather, the mood in the lobby and on the elevator was the rich even luxuriant power of Foreman's fist. He did not just hit hard, he hit in such a way that the nucleus of his opponent's will was reached. Fission began. Consciousness exploded. The head smote the spine with a lightning bolt and the legs came apart like falling walls. On the night Foreman took his championship, who could forget the film of Frazier's urgent legs staggering around the ring, looking for their lost leader?

At the Inter-Continental, there was a prevailing mood then of benign, romantic, even imperial confidence in the power and menace of Foreman. Everybody in his camp was happy. Dick Sadler played with children and flirted with the best-looking women, flirted with droll mastery, never empty of an expression that teased, "Nobody knows the evil you will see." Archie Moore, being introduced to the wife of the American Ambassador in Zaïre, took her immediately by the hand and said, "Come, dear, I want you to meet my wife," and led her to Mrs. Moore. Sandy Saddler, the wise and vicious equal of the great Willie Pep, Sandy still as slim as when he used to fight, would stand to one corner, his small head supporting his large horn-rimmed glasses, looking for all the world like the bitter shrunken proprietor of a pharmacy, and say, "I'm concerned for Ali. I'm afraid he's going to get hurt."

Foreman had a sparring partner named Elmo Henderson, once Heavyweight Champion of Texas. Elmo was tall and thin and did not look like a fighter nearly so much as like some kind of lean wanderer in motley — the long stride of a medieval jester was in his step, and he would walk through the lobby and the patio and around the pool of the Inter-Continental with his eyes in the air as if he sought a vanishing point six feet above the horizon. It gave an envelope to his presence, even a suggestion of silence but this was paradoxical, for Elmo Henderson never stopped talking. It was as if Elmo were Foreman's unheard voice, and the voice was loud. Elmo had learned a Franco-African word, *oyé* (from the French *oyez* — "now hear this") and at whatever hour of the day he went through the lobby or encountered you at Nsele, he was passing through the midst of a continuing inner vision. The voice he heard came from far off and out of a deep source of power — Elmo vibrated to the hum of that distant dynamo. *"Oyé,"* he cried to the world at large in an unbelievably loud and booming voice. *"Oyé . . . oyé . . . ,"* each cry coming in its interval, sometimes so far apart as every ten or fifteen seconds, but penetrating as a dinner gong. Up in the corridors, and on the elevator, out on the taxi entrance of the Inter-Continental and back at the pool, through the buffet tables of the open-air restaurant and all night at the bar, Henderson's cry would come, sometimes in one's ear, sometimes across a floor, *"oyé . . ."* He would stop now and again, as if the signal he transmitted had failed to reach him, then, sudden as the resumption of the chorus of a field of crickets, his voice would twang through the halls. *"Oyé . . . Fore-*

man boma yé . . ." Hear this . . . Foreman will kill him. "*Oyé . . . Foreman boma yé.*" If an expropriation of *Ali boma yé* it was no longer a cry to destroy Sisley High; rather, a call to a crusade. Every time Elmo picked up that chant again, one felt a measure of Foreman's blood beating through the day, pounding through the night in rhythm with the violence that waits through the loneliness of every psychotic aisle. Henderson walked past children and old men, moved by African princes and the officers of corporations here for copper, diamonds, cobalt; his voice took into itself the force of every impulse he passed. Wealth and violence and irritation and innocence were in his voice and to it he added the intensity of his own force until the sound twanged in one's ear like the boom of a cricket grown large as an elephant. "*Oyé . . . Foreman boma yé. . . .*" and Foreman, whether near Henderson or a hundred yards away, seemed confirmed in his serenity by the power of Elmo's throat, as if the sparring partner were the night guard making his rounds, and all was well precisely because all was unwell.

"*Oyé . . . Foreman boma yé,*" Henderson would cry on his tour through the hotel, and once in a while, his face lighting up, as if he had just encountered a variation of the most liberating and prophetic value, he would add, "The flea goes in three, Muhammad Ali," and he would stick three fingers in the air. "*Oyé,*" shouted Henderson one morning in the back of Bill Caplan's ear, and the publicity man for Foreman's camp replied sadly, "Oy vay! Oy vay!" Once Elmo spoke a full sentence. "We're going to get Ali," he said to the lobby at large, "like a Rolls-Royce when we job it up. *Oyé . . . Foreman boma yé.*"

Yes, madness in Africa was fertile, and in this madness of Africa, two fighters would each receive five million dollars while one thousand miles away on the edge of the world-famine Blacks would die of starvation, two fighters each to make more than $100,000 a minute if the fight went the full forty-five minutes and more per minute if it went less. Natural to the madness that one of the fighters was a revolutionary and a conservative, which is to say a Black Muslim, whose ultimate aim was the cession by the United States of a large piece of the United States for the formation of a Black nation, and was, this wealthy revolutionary conservative (a marbles champion at the age of ten) fighting a defender of the capitalist system whose mother had been a cook and a barber and head of a family of seven until she collapsed into a mental hospital and the son confessed at "drunkenness, truancy, vandalism, strong-arm robbery," became a purse-snatcher, and at that — quote Leonard Gardner — "was a total failure; undone by his victims' cries for God's assistance, he was compelled to run back and return all the purses." That was at fourteen, and fifteen, and sixteen. We know the rest of the story. Foreman joins the Job Corps, and wins the Heavyweight title in the Olympics before he is twenty-one. He dances around the ring with a little flag. "Don't talk down the American system to me," he says in full investiture of that flag, "its rewards can be there for anybody if he will make up his mind, bend his back, lean hard into his chores and refuse to allow anything to defeat him. I'll wave that flag in every public place I can," to which Ali would shout at a boxing writers' dinner six years later, "I'm going to beat your Christian ass, you white flag-waving bitch, you." They had grappled on the stage and Ali pulled out Foreman's shirt, left him a man without a shirt wearing a tuxedo. Foreman in return ripped Ali's jacket down the back. There were apologies next day and Ali claimed he would "never insult anyone's religion," but the psychological results were as inconclusive as *Ali boma yé* and *Foreman boma yé;* there was certainly no clear-cut parallel to the afternoon on TV when Ali kept telling Joe Frazier he was ignorant until Frazier attacked him physically. That was just a few days before their second bout, and Ali's insults helped to decide the fight in his favor for Frazier had Ali in trouble through the middle rounds, and looked ready to knock him out by the beginning of the ninth, indeed Ali had just been able to last through a formidable few minutes in the eighth. So sure was Frazier by the beginning of the ninth that he rushed to the middle of the ring before the bell — ignorant, am I? The referee was pushing him back as the bell rang. It gave Ali fifteen extra seconds of rest just when he needed them most. On came the full storm of Frazier's last big attack — ignorant, am I? — but Ali came off the ropes before the end of the ninth to turn the fight — yes, you are ignorant! — and win by a close decision. Ali had been a dean of psychology for that fight. But now such acumen had to be applied to the logic of psychotic guilt, "The flea in three, Muhammad Ali," now the tricks would have to reach into the long vault of the asylum mind, *"oyé, oyé,"* and pick up on the two hundred windows in Houston that Foreman broke because he liked the sound. Was the echo of breaking glass in Foreman's discipline, in the investments of his serenity, yes, estimation was equal to madness, and could

Ali mobilize the two and a half million theater seats in America where followers cheering for him would have to send their cheer up the electronic route in reverse, even as time might yet travel from the future to the past? Ali, grand vizier, now had to mobilize the nation of Zaïre, inchoate nation large as Alaska, Colorado and Texas put together, crazy Kinshasa with its 280,000 eggs, 75,000 pats of butter and 115,000 lumps of sugar all moldering over the thousands of tourists who did not come to the black drumbeating "rumble in the jungle," no sir, no tourist lays out $2000 and more for the chance of getting boiled in a pot in a country where the Belgians left in such haste in 1961 that a *Time* correspondent, Lee Grimes, a man with a genteel, trustworthy face, was given the keys to a house and a car by a man he never saw before and told to live in them and use them as the last words spoken by the Belgian before jumping on the ferry that would buck the clumps of hyacinth to cross the Congo to Brazzaville, safe Brazzaville, safe for this day, and Lee Grimes lived in the Belgian's house, and drove the Belgian's VW until there were sixty-four bullet holes in its skin and the VW would drive no more. Grimes would get past Black sentries in checkpoints on the road by waving his plastic credit cards, Zaïre! a country yet equal in size to all of Austria, Belgium, Britain, Denmark, East Germany, France, Ireland, Italy, Portugal, Spain, Switzerland and West Germany, two hundred groups of languages — two hundred *groups!* — and a literacy rate of thirty-five percent, some said less, a country large as the U.S. east of the Mississippi and with a river now twenty-nine hundred miles long coming down from the most impenetrable mountains and jungle to the sea at Matadi, the Kungo, called the Congo — "Listen to the yell of Leopold's ghost/ Burning in Hell for his hand-maimed host" — the Congo, now the Zaïre. Vachel Lindsay would have wept at the harsh sounds of the vowels in Zye-ear:

THEN I SAW THE CONGO, CREEPING THROUGH THE BLACK,
CUTTING THROUGH THE JUNGLE WITH A GOLDEN TRACK.
Then along that riverbank
A thousand miles
Tattooed cannibals danced in files;
Then I heard the boom of the blood-lust son
And a thigh-bone beating on a tin-pan gong.
And "BLOOD!" screamed the whistles and the fifes of
  the warriors,
"BLOOD!" screamed the skull-faced, lean witch-doctors;
"Whirl ye the deadly voo-doo rattle,
Harry the uplands,
Steal all the cattle,
Rattle-rattle, rattle-rattle, Bing!
Boomlay, boomlay, boomlay, BOOM!"
A roaring, epic, rag-time tune
From the mouth of the Congo
To the mountains of the Moon.

Yes, Congo, now the Zaïre; money of the country, Zaïres; gasoline of the country, Petrol Zaïre; even the cigarettes, Fumez Zaïres. "One Zaïre — one great Zaïre," country that fighters and press and thirty-five fight tourists (out of an expectation of five thousand) would visit after inoculations for cholera, smallpox, typhoid, tetanus, hepatitis — take gamma globulin — not to speak of shots for yellow fever and pills for malaria and Kaopectate in the breach of Leopold's galloping ghost, all titles like "Excellency" or "Most Honorable" abolished, Mobutu known only and modestly as The Guide, The Chief, The Helmsman, The Redeemer, The Father of the Revolution and The Perpetual Defender of Property and People, Mobutu born Joseph Désiré, who now in the deeps of authenticity is called Mobutu Sese Seko Kuku Ngbendu Wa Za Banga — "all-powerful warrior who, because of his endurance and inflexible will to win, will go from conquest to conquest, leaving fire in his wake" — effective translation: "The cock who leaves no chicken intact. Wa Za Banga is up your hole" — yes, Mobutu with his personal 747 and DC-10, his radiotelephone that can call any official in the country and his political past — in 1961, Mobutu transferred Patrice Lumumba to a prison in Katanga where everybody knew they would kill him, and afterward built the monument to martyred Lumumba, highest monument in all of Kinshasa, yes, Le Guide, Le Chef, Le Timonier, Le Rédempteur, and Le Père de la Révolution "is greeted as a savior (everywhere he goes) by squads of gyrating dancers swinging and stamping, waving and winnowing, and all the time singing the President's praises," writes J. J. Grimond for the *New York Times,* and the rich details of his piece will not be quoted in a hurry by the Ministry of National Orientation. "*Foreman boma yé,*" cries Elmo Henderson passing by the patio of the open-air restaurant, and Norman smiles at his guest, a most intelligent American living in Kinshasa for years, adept at several occupations, who has agreed to try to explain this incomparable country (which Ali will seek to mobilize, all collective n'golo and Nommo, all kuntu and muntu — in all the variations of the two hundred groups of languages plus Lingala), yes, will seek, our Muhammad Ali, to bend all forces of the living and dead into the arena of his great *hantu*, that fearful place and time which will come together on four o'clock Wednesday morning in 62,800-seat Stadium of the 20th of May with ten points to the winner of a round and nine or less to the loser, fifteen rounds, with 2000 premier ringside seats at $250 each, not sold, not nearly, but wait for closed circuit to 425 locations in the U.S. and Canada, together with home television live or delayed to 100 countries — our promoters: the Government of Zaïre, Video Techniques, Helmdale Leisure Corporation and Don King Productions, no fewer. Yes, Norman will listen to his guest and smile apologetically (or is it half proudly at Elmo's incantation of God knows what fraction of these African facts and forces — Elmo spelled backwards is Omle: *Oyé Omlé*) and the insanity of mood which is also properly part of every Heavyweight Championship stirs in the hot midday air before the reasonable words of his intelligent guest.

"You see, it's hardly a question of liking Mobutu. No American is going to feel enthusiastic about a man whose head appears out of a cloud every night on national television while the Zaïre anthem is played, but he's not the man to be embarrassed by himself — if you look closely on TV you'll see his tribal staff is in his hand, a man and woman intertwined. It's highly conscious. Africans place emphasis on humans, cosmically speaking — a tribal staff with a man and woman intertwined is an expression of cosmic completeness like Yin and Yang. Mobutu is there to embody men and women in one Zaïre, one consciousness, one source of power — he's already allocated sixty-four million Zaïres, well over one hundred million dollars, for a TV complex that is going to link up every village and hidden tribe he can reach. You know whose face will be on that TV. Why, until recently, Mobutu was the only official name you'd ever see in the papers. When a photo was taken of the President with a few bureaucrats, only his face would be identified. Two weeks ago, the first ambassador to come to Zaïre from Cuba arrived. The papers didn't even mention his name. That, of course, was a relapse to the old methods, but there is no question: Mobutism is Mobutu with all that means, and one thing it certainly means is that unpleasant news won't get out. They had a bad crash with an Air Zaïre plane a few months ago. No word of it in the papers for several days. Then Mobutu indicated that while the accident need not be described, it would be permissible to list the funerals, an indirect species of press freedom if you will.

"Take the name of the country. Why they picked it, we'll never know. Doubtless, our Helmsman liked the sound. He would tend to trust his ear. Besides, Z is the last letter of the alphabet. The last shall be first. So it is announced that is what the country will be called. Then they discover that Zaïre is not an African word. It happens to be Old Portuguese. Be certain, he's not about to admit the error and open himself to ridicule. On the contrary that's probably the moment he decides not only the country but the money and the gasoline and the cigarettes and, for all I know, the contraceptives are going to be called Zaïre. The first rule of dictatorship is reinforce your mistakes.

"It is the same with his prerogatives. He does not need houses in half the capitals of Europe, nor a 747 when his family wants to fly from Brussels to London; to us his incredible display of wealth seems wrong, but for Africans it's another matter. He's the chieftain of the country and a king should wear his robes. It's part of vital force to be resplendent. They would respect him less if his expenses were not larger than life. He's the leader of the nation and so a modern equivalent of president, dictator, monarch, emperor, the chosen of God and *le roi soleil* all in one. Give him the benefit, however, of assuming the chosen of God needs such clout. His problems are beyond measure. Here in Kinshasa itself, the town had three hundred thousand people in 1959, a year before the Belgians left, now the secret figure is a million and a half. The unemployment in this city is forty-eight percent and still people flock in. The reason? Unemployment in rural areas is up to eighty percent. There's a dreadful drought and a fearful shortage of agricultural equipment. Count on it, no Zairois bureaucrat is going to call this country undeveloped. Rather, it's 'underequipped.'

"Add to this unemployment the psychological unrest of thousands of languages, and ten of thousands of tribes among twenty-two million people. All the old traditional ties are breaking up. Everybody is now off the land and off the family. Mobutu becomes the only substitute for the old tradition, the remaining embodiment of the great chief. That is why he won't appear in the stadium on the night of the fight but will see it on closed circuit in his home. Not only because he does not wish to show the world how massive police protection would have to be, but because physically he's not going to be seen under the probe of a TV camera next to Ali and Foreman. God does not stand next to his sons when they are taller.

"But that is the smallest example of his particular sense of how to present himself to his people — if you add up the details, it's not short of genius. On the one hand he is everywhere, the boldest presentation of ego one can conceive; on the other, he is endlessly cautious. He produces the fight and the stadium as gifts to his people, but will not appear himself. So you will see him on television every night, you will never get a private interview. His pride is to control his details.

"For example, you will hear everywhere you ask that the army is the base of his power, and it is. One reason is that the price of beer is kept low for soldiers, a detail, but he is meticulous about details. He knows where every officer in his army is posted — he is careful that no important officer is ever in command of troops from his own tribe. Soldiers cannot even speak each other's languages. They must address each other in Lingala. So he insures two things. His power base is not going to be eroded by tribal rebellions, and his soldiers will tend to lose their own dialect and pick up the national tongue. Something similar is done with high government officials. He will take an important man who grew up in Kinshasa and post him as governor of Lubumbashi — this discourages thoughts of a coup. Of course, Mobutu pays a price. The efficiency of the country is not to be described. It has progressed from the intolerable to the dreadful. On the other hand, he inherited such trouble from the Belgians. The bureaucracy was always a fudge factory guaranteed to slow up every top technician the country imports. Now, with the white man out, nobody is going to leap to obey orders. Moreover, think of the kind of white man who came here from Belgium in the first place, not able to cut it in the mainland and taking it out on the Blacks down here, no, paralysis has always been the rule in the middle of the bureaucracy. Indeed, each little office tends to be a tribe. If I have my small job and need an assistant, I hire my kinsman. To avoid treachery. I do not want the new man to steal my job, and if he is in my family he is less likely to think that way. On the other hand, my kinsman is stupid so I do not delegate authority to him or he will get me in trouble. Everything has to wait until I do it. A fudge factory. Nothing moves in the middle levels of the bureaucracy. All the while there's talent at the top, real talent, real intelligence. They are the best educated Blacks, back from Europe with good salaries, good homes, European wives — a mark of pride among top bureaucrats is to have white wives — and they are loyal to Mobutu. It's a good country for them. They can even get things done so long as they are working among themselves. The moment, however, a project has to descend to the middle regions of the administration, we're back in the fudge. Stasis and chaos. 'Pas de problème,' they will dependably say when you ask if something can be arranged. It is their way of guaranteeing that your request is next to hopeless. Since the solution does not exist, neither does the problem. *'Pas de problème.'*

"Yet Mobutu has the country functioning. With waste one does not even wish to conceive and with an official rip-off of natural resources nobody can begin to estimate, the country is nonetheless emerging. Black power is talked about everywhere — it is in some fashion actually being practiced here. Somewhere in the middle of all this, there may even be an idea — the marriage of modern technology with elements of African tradition. This is not because Mobutu is necessarily a wise and profound man — who could begin to know the answer to that when he is not to be approached? — but there may be some instinct in the Congo that technology will never work if it cannot be connected to the African root.

"Still, what a horror," said the brilliant American, echoing Conrad's terminal word. "You are going tonight to see the weigh-in. Take a good look at the stadium. It is Mobutu's gift to the people, built out of their work and their taxes. An amazing structure. The best laborers in Zaïre have been assigned to the stadium. Mobutu has a few skilled cadres of workmen, and he moves them around from one hot spot in the construction of the economy to the next. So we know where they were working these last few months. What a stadium! Do not ignore the design. It is not just a place for receiving people but for processing them, and, if necessary, disposing of them. Late last spring, the crime wave grew so intense that thieves were posing as policemen. The wives of Americans were getting raped. A nightmare for Mobutu if foreigners should arrive for the fight and get mugged en masse. So his police round up in a hurry three hundred of the worst criminals they can find and lock them in some of the holding rooms under the stadium. Then fifty of the three hundred were killed. Right there on the stone floor under the stadium. For all we know, some of them could have been shot in the dressing rooms of the fighters. The key to the execution was that it took place at random. No one bothered to list them. No one said, "Kill this particular fifty." No, they just eliminated the nearest fifty. The random destruction was more desirable. Fear among the criminal population would then go deeper. Good connections with the police are worthless in such an unstructured situation. For much the same reason the other two hundred and fifty criminals were let go. So they would tell their friends of the massacre. The crime rate for this brief period is down. Mobutism. Mayor, tycoon and tyrant at once. He'll spend millions to develop off-shore oil resources where Zaïre has only twenty-three miles on the Atlantic coast, yet he'll succeed — to everyone's surprise, he'll succeed, he'll develop enough oil for his domestic requirements. Then he'll pick up the phone and inquire about an increase in taxi fares in some town eight hundred miles east of Kinshasa and tell them they can't have the raise. Bold, trivial and imperial — an African mind. Africa is shaped like a pistol, say the people here, and Zaïre is the trigger. Enjoy the stadium."

There were weigh-ins that gave a clue to the outcome, but they usually took place the morning of the bout, and thereby could reveal how the fighters had slept. Tonight, however, was Saturday — the contest more than seventy-two hours off. The weigh-in would be no more than publicity, a swatch of electronic space for "Wide World of Sports" on late Saturday afternoon back in the States; it had to be intrinsically boring despite the thousands of Zairois invited free to the stadium.

The expectation of the press was that the crowds would cheer wildly for Ali but there was little excitement — more a firm round of applause — and the ovation for Foreman while smaller was still comparable, perhaps half as large. When all was said, the audience seemed indifferent. What with the crowd of a hundred or more people jamming the ring, the fighters could hardly be seen. Some of the men and women in the stands had been waiting a long time. Besides, it is not precisely breathtaking for a Heavyweight to get on a scale; the greatest excitement, tonight, came from an error. Ali's weight was announced as 206 pounds. He had not been so low in years: 216 pounds came through as the correction. A miscalculation of the kilos. A whistle from the press. He was four to eight pounds heavier than he had said he would be, a poor prospect for his ability to dance and run. In fact, he was almost as heavy as Foreman, who weighed in at 220 pounds, and stood in the ring with full concentration. He was not hearing a sound he did not wish to hear.

Ali looked sullen again. He had come through the ropes with an ivory walking stick, and had seemed more interested in the cane than his surroundings. He handled the stick with quietly inquiring fingers — Ali had a way with new objects — something in his fingers always respected them. The response of the crowd, however, could hardly please him. He led a cheer, "*Ali boma yé*," but there was nothing overpowering in the response.

Meanwhile, music played. It was disconcertingly happy music, as rippling as Carribbean rhythms — music for the hips, no character necessary, only a loose spine. You did not hear the fell thonk of fisticuffs in the music, yes, a curious disappointment, the weigh-in, even the ring was too low. Just as they had installed it too high at Nsele, so was it now much too low. The photographers standing at the apron would block the view of the reporters at the press tables. Everybody would be standing.

In truth, it was not a happy stadium. One's intelligent American informant had been correct. The entrance was depressing in the extreme. It was not a place for people to enter; rather, an edifice from which it was impossible to exit if the police wished to retain you. The rate of flow suggested a beer keg with a baby's nipple for a spigot. From the street, arches no wider than ordinary doors opened to turnstiles, which in turn allowed you to pass along through narrow corridors to the stadium seats. Off an underground passageway that ran in an oval around the stadium were rooms of cement-brick painted entirely in gray. Steel bars and cinder block. A prison.

The mood provided by the weigh-in was still on Norman when he joined a party in the bar on the top floor of the Inter-Continental. There Don King was celebrating the same weigh-in. For King, it had been a milestone. He was happy to announce it in just that way. "Tonight, seeing Ali and Foreman in the ring, I can believe in the reality of this fight," he said.

King had magical eyes. Until one met him, it was hard to understand how he could possibly have managed to bring the fighters together, for he had few financial resources to match an event of this scope. King, however, had the ability to take all his true love (which given his substantial Black presence was not necessarily small) plus all of his false love, and pour them out together through his eyes, his lambent eyes. Mailer had never believed in the real existence out in the field of the word lambent but then he had never looked before into a pair of eyes as full of love. "You are a genius in tune with the higher consciousness," King offered as the first compliment on meeting, "yet an instinctive exponent of the untiring search for aspiration in the warm earth-embracing potential of exploited peoples." Norman had once known a Rumanian doctor with just such a mouth-filling taste for rhetoric and pastrami. Don King was a cross between a Negro Heavyweight large as Ernie Terrell and that Jewish Rumanian doctor, nay, King was even B'nai Brith-ical. He could not say *ecstatic* if you did not let him add *with delight*. Occasions were never joyous if they could be *very joyous*. After a while Mailer realized that the description of himself offered with such generosity by King was in fact a way of letting you in on King's view of himself — "a genius in tune with the higher consciousness," et cetera.

Say, it would be hard to prove King was not a genius. A former nightclub owner and numbers king of Cleveland with four years in jail for killing a man in a street fight, he had approached Ali and Foreman with the splendid credentials of a fight manager whose two best fighters, Earnie Shavers and Jeff Merritt, had just both been knocked out in the first round. Still, he offered to promote Ali-Foreman. Each fighter would get five million dollars, he said. Those eyes of true love must have made the sum believable, for they glowed doubtless with the cool delights of lemonade, the fantasies of Pernod, and the golden kernels of corn — somehow, those eyes took him through barriers — he convinced Herbert Muhammad that he could produce this fight. "I reminded him of the teaching of his father Elijah Muhammad that every qualified Black man should be given a chance by his fellow Black men." Of course, the more cynical were quick to point out that Herbert Muhammad had little to lose — King was quickly locked into a contract where he had to pay $100,000 a month every month until a letter of credit for the $10,000,000 was in the bank for both fighters, and King, to everybody's surprise, managed to hang on long enough to raise the money through John Daly of Helmdale Leisure Corp, and Risnailia, a Swiss corporation whose heart belonged, it was said, to Sese Seko Kuku Ngbendu Wa Za Banga, our own Mobutu. What skills. Quantity changes quality, Engels said once, and a hustler of dimensions is a financier. How King could talk. He was a tall man, but his graying hair stood up four inches from his head, straight up, straight up — he was one Black whose Afro was electrified by a perpetually falling elevator — *whoosh* went the hair up from his head. Down came his words. King wore diamonds and pleated shirts, dashikis with gold pendants, powder-blue tuxedos and suits of lipstick-red; the cummerbunds of a sultan were about his waist, and the pearls of the Orient in the cloth he wore. How he could talk. He was the kuntu of full dialogue, and no verbal situation could be foreign to him. Once when one of his lesser-known fighters hinted that a contract was unsatisfactory and King could get hurt, Don leaned forward — fond was he of telling this story — and said, "Let us not bullshit each other. You can leave here, make a call, and have me killed in half an hour. I can pick up the phone as you leave and have you offed in five minutes." That was expression appropriate to the point, but King could cut a wider path. "The fight," he said, "will draw a trillion fans, because Ali is Russian, Ali is Oriental, Ali is Arabic, Ali is Jewish, Ali is everything that one could conceive with the human mind. He appeals to all segments of our world. Some polarize themselves with hostility and affection, but regardless he stimulates — and this is the most significant part — Ali motivates even the dead." Yes, even the dead who were dying of thirst and waiting for beer at the altar. "The dead tremble in their graves" was what King said as Leonard Gardner reported it in Caracas on the night Foreman annihilated Norton and the last impediment to Ali-Foreman was gone. King had been happy that night, and he was happy this night with the weigh-in staged and the television satellite tested and proved. He was a man who obviously placed serious investments of faith in formal ceremony, and that same stadium which proved so sinister to his guest brought tears to King's eyes as he spoke of it. "Tonight has been a culmination," he said. "Tonight the history of our problems on this fight become converted to the history of our hardworking triumphs. I had a vision tonight of the event to come and it leaves me ebullient for I see an encounter that will be without compare in the relentless power of its tenacity and fury. Therefore it occasions in me the emotion that I am an instrument of eternal forces."

Once you became accustomed to the stately seesaw of his rhetoric it gave nourishment to your ear the way a Cossack's horse in full stride would give drumbeats to the steppes. Still, it became evident after a while that King whipped his tongue for rhetoric when he did not have a finer reply. (As Shaw once assured Sam Goldwyn, poetry was there to write when he did not feel inspired for prose.) So King shifted gears whenever the beginnings of a small distance were sensed between himself and the person to whom he spoke; when he rapped, however, ah, then King became the other man in himself.

He liked to talk about his four years in prison and his five unsuccessful appearances before a parole board. "My past was jamming me with those people, you see. I had to put in the years, had to learn how to rechannel myself, and be able to meditate in a room full of violent men. No easy task. It was sheer hell just to go to the hole. You could wake up in the middle of the night and have to take a leak. What a sight in the urinals. Prisoners sucking guards. Guards going down on prisoners. One man taking another's ass. Hell, man, you got to get your head in order."

At the next table, Hunter Thompson leaned over to John Vinocur and said, "Bad Genet."

"I decided to study," said King. "I got myself a list. Got my education in prison. Read Freud. He almost blew my mind. Breast, penis, anus. Powerful stuff. Then Masters and Johnson, Kinsey, and . . ." He hesitated. "Knee's itch, I read a lot of him."

"Who?"

"Knee's itch. Nigh zith."

"Nietzsche?"

"Yeah." But the error had him jiving for embarrassment. "Yeah, cerebrum and cerebellum, you got to use them, that's what I learned from that man."

"Who else did you read?"

"Kant — *The Critique of Pure Reason.* That helped my head. And I read Sartre — fascinating! — and then the guy who wrote the book on Hitler, Shirer, I read him. And Marx, I read Karl Marx, a cold motherfucker, Marx. I learned a lot from him. Hitler and Marx — I think of them in relation to some of the things they're doing here, you know, the country is the family. Concentrate on the young."

At the next table, Hunter Thompson having finished his drink, said, "Very bad Genet."

But King did not hear him. Why should King care? He had probably read Genet. The fatigue and happiness of the thousand perils of successfully promoting this fight sat in kindly weight upon his back. "Yes," he said, "I look upon tonight as a classically satisfying experience."

9. KING OF THE FLUNKIES

HUNTER THOMPSON was tall and had the rangy build of a college halfback from a small school. Although he was half-bald and a little over thirty, he never lost that look. He could be suffering physical agony but he never appeared in more pain than showed on his high forehead, which was usually full of the dew of a quiet sweat. He perspired. That was the sole price he seemed to pay for swallowing more chemicals to bring him up and take him down than any good living writer. He could probably drink more beer than all but a hundred men alive. He obviously possessed a memorable constitution. By now, however, he was so strung out that he squeaked if you poked a finger near his belly. He was a set of nerves balanced on another set of nerves traveling on squeaky roller skates. Here to cover the fight for *Rolling Stone,* he hated the heavenly raptures of all who were here to be happy for the fight. He hated the assignment. Hunter took one look at Kinshasa and tried to charter a plane to Brazzaville.

He could not, of course, find a plane. The national

disaster of Zaïre was not speaking to the civic disaster of Brazzaville. Three days before the fight, Hunter still had the expression on his face of having already written the story from Brazzaville. He was in a state of high shock. He looked like a halfback who has just been tackled in the neck and is walking on his toes. In the bar at the top of the Inter-Continental, he said, "Bad Genet" with the ingenuous "Zowie" of a protagonist who is hearing unutterable sounds of collision in his head, throat, and gullet as beer and froth collide.

When Mailer thought about Don King, it was with Hunter Thompson's remark, "Bad Genet." Never did materials seem more ready for the sensational repudiation Hunter could give to organized madness. Yet any good writer knew satire would violate too much here. It was like coming onto a goldfield and discovering your glints were not gold but foodstuff, half horse manure, half yellow manna. If King had been a white man, what a stentorian job one could do — a hustler with straight genius for the vulgar. Recognize him as Black and he was a genius with a hustle, one more embodiment of that organic philosophy walking in now, centuries late, from the savannah and the rain forest. The technological world, wandering along in the confusion of a rationality which had run the railroad off the tracks, might be in need of Black culture. "Ali even motivates the dead," said King, and was talking of natural human powers. Some men have it more than others. Ali has it. He motivates the dead. An uncommon but not unrealistic ability.

Of course, Don King, unknown to himself, could be

wrapped in the same philosophical cloth as Ogotemmêli. Each human is born, says our Dogon sage, with two souls: one of male and one of female sex — two distinct persons to inhabit each body. A man's female soul will be found in the foreskin; the woman's private male lives in the clitoris. Back to *The Politics of Sex*. Don King, reading Freud, could feel his unconscious acting up to a few concepts of a lost culture he did not know he possessed. "Breast, penis, anus. Powerful stuff. Integral."

Black motivation was not white motivation. Absurdity to the white was white meat for the Black. In Africa, Norman would try to observe with two eyes instead of one.

Conceivably he had first to observe himself. That night, after drinking with King, Norman found himself on the balcony of his room. Maybe it was in the original design, or perhaps the railings had gone up in price before the Inter-Continental was done, but every room had an architectural conceit — its balcony was without a railing. Call it not a balcony but a shelf. One could get on it by sliding open the big window in the room. The shelf ran for the width of the room, twelve feet wide more or less, and stuck out three feet from the window to the lip. From the unprotected lip, you could look down into a fall of seven stories.

On each side of the shelf was a partitioning wall of concrete flush with the shelf; it was also three feet in width but ran from floor to ceiling. Perhaps its function was to restrain a prowler from walking along the shelf to a stranger's window.

Of course, it had not taken long to realize that the partition might be no more than an ideological restraint. One could step around that side wall onto the next shelf. It would be necessary to lean out as you did it, and there would be nothing to hold onto for that moment but both sides of the partition. Those sides were six inches apart, palm to palm, which is to say, six inches thick. Holding on that way, you could conceivably rear backward, lose your grip, and fall. It was not likely, of course. You would have to lean out very far before your hands (pressed firmly, we may be certain, to both sides of the wall) would fail to hold. Probably no physical feat was involved. Nonetheless, the chance to whirl around that wall over to the next balcony offered vertigo. How ridiculous a way to get yourself killed. What could be worse than accidental suicide? A reverberation of Hemingway's end shivered its echo. Once Norman had climbed up a ladder in the studio of a man who had died the season before. His heart beating ridiculously on that folding ladder, he mounted from the penultimate rung to the top. There, on the top rung, his body quivered back and forth like a tuning fork. He was caught in a current which had nothing to do with him. He had climbed the mast into a squall of magical forces. With what trembling he climbed down. He had reason to fear. Once, a little earlier in that same period of his life, while covering the second Ali-Liston fight, then scheduled for Boston, he had been miserable for days before forcing himself to take a short walk on a parapet. The parapet was a foot wide and required no exceptional sense of balance. Still it was fifteen steps along the edge of a roof of a high old building in Beacon Hill. He had been sick for days with the imperative to do it. Finally, he did it. One hour later, Ali's groin muscles tore. The fight was called off for months. How could you ever know with clarity whether the walk on the roof had been connected or absolutely unconnected to Ali's rupture? A small obsession for a magician.

Now, these last few days, he had been passing through similar temptations. A Heavyweight Championship was a vortex; not surprising to get into the whirl. But for years he had been trying to avoid stunts. They were too removed from the daily ability to live with a reasonable balance between one's courage and one's fear; these private capers were out of measure. He knew he could slip around the partition. But what if he were visited by the involuntary trembling he felt on top of the ladder that summer day a decade ago? So he kept the possibility of going around the wall to the next balcony as a possibility he was simply not going to entertain. On the consequence of this thought he felt disloyal to Ali. He knew Muhammad's chances would be greater if he did it than if he didn't. And was furious at the vanity. Ali did not need his paltry magic — "Ali even motivates the dead." Of course, considering Foreman, Ali might need all the help he could get.

On this Saturday night, long after the weigh-in, not dead drunk, but good and drunk, his mind clear, his limbs functioning as neatly as one can drive a car neatly when deep in drink, he came back to the room, opened his window without ado, stepped out on the balcony — it was 4 A.M. Sunday morning — put his hands on each side of the partition, worked around to the next balcony, nodded, swung back to his own balcony, performed much the same crossing to the balcony on the other side, nodded again, came back, climbed through the window, got into bed, and before falling asleep, had time to say to himself, "It was so fucking easy."

Of course he had done it all in freedom from fear. The freedom that drinking brings. By the logic of magical equations, it was conceivable he had reversed the signs; to be drunk might be to reverse all signs. You could be working for the opposite of what you intend. So in the morning he did not have the remotest idea whether he had brought aid and comfort to the Muslims or the Foremans; he almost did not care. A modest element in this oncoming collision, he must have been picked up by forces he could find familiar but hardly comprehend. A Heavyweight Championship is as charged as a magnetic field. So he did not have the remotest doubt of his own sanity, just the rueful sensation of being tickled by magical tides he would never see.

Downstairs, on this Sunday morning, Bundini was having a war with Elmo. "*Oyé . . . Foreman boma yé . . .*" had been dominating the lobby too long. Bundini had gone into the lists for his boss. A crowd was gathered around Bundini and Elmo, who stood three feet apart, sure measure it was unwise to come nose to nose. Each man kept talking. It was not a flurry of sound but a melee — their voices clanged. "Your fighter is untutored, can't move his head. My man is going to stick him till he's bleeding and dead," shouted Bundini. Having slammed his logic from rhyme to rhyme, he added, "God is going to leave him infirm, wailing like a worm, feed him a cabbage leaf, sucker!"

Elmo, unperturbed, stuck up three fingers, and held them in Bundini's face. Elmo would spear a thrice-noxious orifice: two nostrils and a big mouth. "The flea," said Elmo with all solemnity, "goes in three. Muhammad Ali."

In the circle about the two men, just about everybody was working for Foreman. They laughed, *Foreman boma yé, Foreman boma yé,*" Henderson kept repeating to everything Bundini said at a volume just larger than the voice that shouted back. Bundini's voice grew hoarse, his language was obscured. Pressure was certainly upon him. Back of Henderson, six feet back, his head in a book, stood Foreman. His huge police dog, Daggo, raised in George's own kennels, stood next to him. On every side were sparring partners and members of the retinue. Each time Bundini began to speak, they would shout him down. "Bullshit," they would cry. Henderson's tongue would state: "The flea in three." It was getting expensive for Bundini to pause. "Ali, the flea, he dead in three. *Oyé,*" boomed Elmo, "*Oyé!*"

"You call that a sound?" roared Bundini, "*oyé?*" his eyes bulging out of his head. His eyes looked ready to be extruded from the skull. Plop would they fall to the floor.

"Foreman hits Ali. Muhammad is dead," Elmo said.

"He'll never hit him. My man will dance. My man will know how to prance. He's a genius, he's a god, your man's a pug. Foreman'll be looking for the rug. We'll let him squirm," said Bundini, his voice getting thinner, "*Ali boma yé.*" Catcalls and whistles.

"The flea in three," said Elmo solemnly.

"Put your money where your mouth is," Bundini screamed. He whipped the last of his vocal cords. "I got a man in my corner ready to fight. I'm ready to go with him. Who do you have? Your man's got a dog for a pet, and a nut for a companion."

Foreman looked up for the first time and the dog looked up with him. Foreman put his face back resolutely in the book. But a wave came off. It was succinct. "Kidding is kidding," said the wave, "but get your ass off my pillow."

There were too many people working for Foreman. There was something tireless in the voice of Elmo Henderson. Bundini, bruising the air with his eyeballs, started heading for the elevator. He might have been hoping to extract the wrong turf. Elmo stuck with him, however, the sparring partners stuck, they all stuck with him on the move across that electric carpet. About ten large Black men piled into the elevator with Bundini. His voice slammed shut in the clanging of the gate. Images of mayhem rose in the mind — who could not see shreds and splinters of Bundini?

Still, in the evening, there was Bundini, eating in the restaurant on the open-air patio with his wife, Shere, a white girl from Texas with red hair, green eyes, a stubborn upturned nose, and a Down Home accent. Shere (pronounced Sherry or Cherie) looked as American as the boy with freckles whose face is on the box of breakfast food. Bundini kept calling her "Mother." She called him by his first name, Drew, for Drew "Bundini" Brown.

Mailer was confused. The last time he had seen much of Bundini was years ago, and Bundini was married then to a Jewish girl. His son, he was proud to tell everyone, had been bar mitzvah. A tall good-looking young black boy with curly Jewish hair, Drew Brown, Jr., used to greet Bun-

dini's Jewish friends with "Sholom, aleichom sholom." To
Black friends the boy would remark, "Begin running,
motherfucker."

Once, almost ten years ago, in Las Vegas for the Ali-
Patterson fight, Mailer and Bundini had done some drinking together. At the time Bundini had been fired by Ali
for some undescribed misdeed. It was obvious he still had
much feeling for Ali, but if your man has chosen to reject
you, the logic of hustling is to work against him. So Bundini was looking for a connection to Patterson. He knew,
after all, every one of Ali's weaknesses. Patterson, however,
would not let Bundini near. Patterson did not trust him.
Bundini, with the aid of George Plimpton, had to be con-
tent therefore with writing a neat piece for *Life* that gave
open advice on the best tactics available to Patterson. Since
Floyd's back went out in the second round, and he fought
in all the pain of a slipped disk and a muscle spasm, a
brave but wholly miserable encounter, Bundini's tip — that
Patterson should crowd Ali as in a street fight, which
proved to be exactly what Frazier would do six years later
— proved academic. But then Bundini was down on his
luck all over that year — there was nobody to whom he
didn't owe money.

In compensation, Bundini was never more likable. His
eyes could send almost as much love as Don King's and his
voice grew as husky as the germination of thought itself.
Bundini could neither read nor write — so he claimed —
but he could speak. It was rare for him to make a remark
void of metaphor. On the Ali-Foreman fight he commented
to the press, "God set it up this way. This is the closing of

the book. The king gained his throne by killing a monster and the king will regain his throne by killing a bigger monster. This is the closing of the book." Of training he would propose, "You got to get the hard-on, and then you got to keep it. You want to be careful not to lose the hard-on, and cautious not to come." Of George Plimpton, who lent him money in the period when he was banished from Ali's camp, Bundini said, "I'll always be loyal to George, because he took care of me when my lips was chapped."

Norman and Bundini might have become friends — the writer respected the style with which Bundini could pass through trouble. At a time when collection men were getting ready to break his legs, Bundini would drop his last four hundred dollars on eight rolls of the dice and walk away with a sad wise smile. Like many a hustler he was *sweet*. He could cry like a child — indeed he cried whenever Ali boxed with beauty, cried at the bounty of the Lord to provide such athletic bliss — and his eyes beamed with love at any remark that excited his own powers of metaphor. Then his big round face would show the simple happiness of Aunt Jemima, his big husky voice would croon in admiration at such wonders of wisdom. That was half of him; Bundini was just as proud of his other soul. If he was all emotion, he could show his ice; if he had class, he could be without class; he'd give his life for a friend and you might believe him, but "he would," said a critic, "take the dimes off a dead man's eyes and put nickels back." Small surprise if he had a build like nobody else. Over six feet with a big crystal ball for a head, he had small shoulders, a small protruding stomach that seemed to center its melon on his diaphragm, and spindles for legs — it was the body of a spaceman who grew up in a capsule. Yet he had fought in Navy competitions as an adolescent; even now nobody would take Bundini on for too little (except Ali, who slapped him at will as though dealing with an unregenerate child). Bundini was plain as a mouthful of gold teeth and handsome as black velvet; if he called his young wife "Mother," he had been about as fatherly in his day as any other player: a magazine story once spoke of his desire to be a "marketable pimp." But then he sold interviews of himself which told it all, and gave metaphors away for nothing; he could not spell a word and had a dozen movie scripts he was trying to sell, his own, he claimed. Recall us to "Float like a butterfly, sting like a bee." Bundini was the walking definition of the idea that each human is born with two souls — two distinct persons to inhabit each body. If Africans did not have the concept, one would have to invent it. What a clash of Nommo and n'golo. All that spirit, all that prick. The two never came together. After a while, Norman and he were no longer friends. Their fight was serious enough not to speak for years. But the fight game shakes old prejudices like castanets. Since he and Bundini kept being thrown together at fights, and since Bundini kept helping him in little ways whether he wished it or not, they finally began to talk a little, if more than a little on guard. For years they talked to each other just a little.

This fight, Bundini was shifting the terms. One afternoon, just as Norman was walking down the bank of the Zaïre after a visit with Ali, he heard a voice shout to him from a neighboring villa.

"Hey, No'min, come here."

The tone was not pleasant, but he was curious who was calling. Somewhat too late, he realized he was approaching Bundini, who stood in the vestibule of the villa surrounded by a group of Black friends. He had been drinking. Straight out, he was drunk. It was easy to tell with Bundini. The whites of his eyes turned egg-yolk yellow and blooded with webs of red. His breath smelled of the vats.

"I learned," he declared to Norman, "the meaning of my name in African today. I've been blessed. What you been blessed with?"

"Meeting you."

"You talking like I'm still a nigger. Niggers is yesterday. I've been blessed with the root. I'm in harmony. What you been blessed with?" he asked once more. Bundini was warming up to play the dozens. "Show me your blessing," he said, "show me your blessing." The dozens, no mistake. Other Blacks were grinning with the possibilities.

"I'm blessed with listening to you beat your gums." Hardly a good reply. Points were already accumulating to Bundini.

"My black gums are dark with the misery and the wonder. The jewels of oppression are shining in my black gums, motherfucker."

"You speaking of your black bar mitzvah gums?"

No smiles from the audience. Bundini was treating him like a stranger. "I learned my black name today," he said, "I learned what Bundini means."

"What does it mean?" The answer was weak. You did not parley the dozens, you brought forth an onslaught.

131

"Bundini means I'm back in the blood of my people. I'm the steeple. I'm the point of it all. My black heart is beautiful. Bundini! *Something like dark* is what they say Bundini means. *Something like dark*," said Bundini, going back over the translation with relish.

"*Not quite dark* is what it means." For the first time the Blacks around Bundini laughed a little.

"You're just envious," said Bundini, "because you don't have a name in African, motherfucker. You have none of the black juice. The berries in your belly are pale. Your blood is in jail, motherfucker. As you shit, you mumble, you're afraid of the jungle. You're afraid of the jungle, motherfucker!"

"I just wish my mother was here," Norman managed to say, "because if she was, she would give you a whupping!"

Maybe his voice caught something of Ali's tone, or maybe it had just gone on long enough, but everybody burst into laughter, and Bundini smote his hand as if he was now Honorary Black. On the round of good feeling this had to offer, Norman also felt some large part of unforgiveness to Bundini begin to lift. Only afterward did it occur to him that drunk in the middle of the afternoon, Bundini was still wise enough to choose the dozens as a way of reestablishing relations, certainly wise enough to thrust victory upon him.

So this night, passing Bundini's table where he sat with Shere, it was impossible to refuse his offer of a drink. Before too long, Norman accepted his invitation to dinner, and wondered what Bundini had in mind for he kept going over to other tables to advance his business interests, which were numerous, various, in process, and secret. Shere made conversation with Norman about the ivory market, apartments in New York, her children, and these weeks of missing them, and finally they spoke of the absence of white women out at Nsele, which had been the reason for her desire to move to the Inter-Continental. "It got so I couldn't put on a swimsuit without creating a near riot." Truth, she had the figure to do that, but something strong and determined in her features would take no pleasure from such brouhaha. "At Nsele I just stayed in my room. Drew was out working with Ali, so what did he know, but I was going crazy. It's much better here."

Drew eventually came back. He was alternately surly and meek with his wife. He was preoccupied. He asked about Ali's mood, and they talked about that for a while since Norman had spent the afternoon with Ali at Nsele. It had been a curious Sunday. Ali's voice had left him. Whether it was the cold that appeared to be coming on the night they ran or simple laryngitis from talking too much, Ali could offer no more than a hoarse whisper, a frightening prospect for the fight if his voice was the measure of his strength. But he certainly seemed happy enough. At twilight, he took a walk on the banks of the river, and was surrounded by hundreds of Zairois men, women, and children. He kissed babies and had his picture taken with numbers of black and jubilant housewives in African Sunday dress, and with shy adolescent girls, and little boys who glared at the camera with machismo equal to the significance of these historic events. All the while Ali kissed babies with deliberation, slowly, savoring their skin, as if he could divine which infants would grow up healthy. He was one politician who would love kissing babies.

Back inside the villa with friends and family for company, he kept speaking in a strained small tone. "Don't talk too much," Pat Patterson kept telling him. "Rest your voice."

Ali shrugged. "Oh, I got to talk," he said. "I'd die if I couldn't talk. But I'll be careful not to say too much."

He began watching TV cassettes of Foreman's fights. It was a curious half hour of early evening. Mrs. Clay was there, and she was a plump and very handsome woman with a light skin, a Southern lady, just about, indeed, she looked like a matronly version of Julie Eisenhower, or more properly, let us say we can see the way Julie Eisenhower may look when she is the age of Ali's mother. Now as Ali watched the Frazier-Foreman fight, his mother sat on the other side of the living room and watched with him. Once more, George appeared in his red trunks and proceeded to demolish Frazier, once more the sledgehammering punches went bouncing off Frazier's brain. Again came the sight of Frazier's face as he got up in the first round looking like a man on whom a wall has just fallen. He is back on his feet but the sky is shocking in its tilt.

As Frazier went down for the third time and Foreman, in his red trunks, stepped away, Mrs. Clay said, "That's going to be Ali in the red trunks."

Ali watched the films in an odd good mood as if there were something he saw that he would certainly use two nights from now. The fight with José Roman in Tokyo was shown next, a fight in which Roman threw a total of six punches before Foreman threw one. None of Roman's punches reached Foreman. Foreman then threw twenty-four punches to Roman's three. More than half of Foreman's punches landed. He smashed through Roman's arms to reach his body. Roman, lying on the floor, had the glitter of a dying animal in his eye. Then a cassette of the Foreman-Norton fight. In all, Ali watched three fights with Foreman, a total of five rounds and twelve knockdowns. He looked pleased. Something he had seen. Something he could use. Who could know what it was? Each time Foreman knocked a man out, frustration showed on his face. Foreman looked like he still wanted to kill them.

Bundini, having listened to Norman's account, now nodded somberly, and said across the table, "Jesus has no fear."

"Do you mean Allah has no fear?"

"I call Allah Jesus. It all comes out of God. Whatever you call Him. My man is right there with Jesus, Allah, Jehovah. He's got it all."

Slowly, the motive for Bundini's invitation to dinner emerged. He wanted Norman to look at his scripts and advise him.

"But I thought you can't read or write."

"I can't. But I can talk. People took down my words. I want you to take down some of my words."

"Drew — why don't you learn to write? You can do it. It's time."

Bundini looked serious and very sad. "I'm afraid to," he said. "I learned what I learned not knowing how to read, not knowing how to write. My strength is in the same place as Samson's hair. Reading and writing is Delilah to me. I don't want to lose the magic God alone gave me. I got to fight for my boy," he said. "He's in there to fight. I got to be there too." He offered one fine confidence. "I'm sharpening the spike. I'm going to give Foreman's people the needle tonight."

"How do you do that?"

"Oh, I'm going up to them to put some money on Ali. But I won't ask for 3 to 1. I'm going to give two thousand dollars against their three. That got to worry them. They be wondering where I get the confidence. It go right back to George Foreman."

"You have a real two thousand dollars?"

"Better be real!"

They laughed.

And so in the middle of the same lobby where Bundini had been outshouted by Elmo Henderson on Sunday morning, Bundini returned to joust on Sunday night. Elmo was not about. For certain, Bundini must have picked a time when Elmo was not about.

Having attracted some of Foreman's people, the sparring partner Stan Ward among them, Bundini began to jeer. "I don't want 3 to 1, I don't need 3 to 1. *My* man is 3 to 1."

"Then give *us* 3 to 1," said Stan Ward.

"I would. If God was here, I would. But He ain't. He don't associate with flunkies who work for George Foreman, that big man, that big white man. I don't give you 3 to 1 because I don't give no advantage to people who work for the White Man."

"Then why you asking 3 to 2 instead of 3 to 1," someone said suspiciously.

"Because you the bullies. Anybody works for the White Man is a bully. A bully needs advantage. I'm giving you advantage. You go out in the casinos and try to get your bet. You have to lay three to get one. You people are too fucking scared to do that. 'Cause you know the White Man upstairs. You know his faults. You know you going to lose."

"Foreman ain't going to lose," said Stan Ward.

"Give me *your* bet," said Bundini.

"How much you laying?"

"My two thousand dollars is in my hands," said Bundini pulling out a roll. "Now show me, nigger, where your three thousand dollars is."

"I can't get it right away," said Ward. "But I'll have it in the morning. I'll meet you here at eleven in the morning."

"Yeah, if the White Man tells you to go ahead and pee, then you can piss," said Bundini.

"He ain't the White Man."

"Shit, he ain't. There he is in the Olympics, a big fat fool dancing around with an eentsy American flag in his big dumb fist. He don't know what to do with a fist. My man does. My man got his fist in the air when he wins. Power to the People! That's my man. Millions follow him. Who follows your man? He's got nobody to follow him," said Bundini, "that's why he keeps a *dog*." The followers of Foreman suddenly roared with happiness. The kuntu was audacity and they paid their respects to the spirit of audacity embodied in Bundini. "What are you ready to die for?" asked Bundini. He answered them, "Nothing. You

137

ain't ready for nothing. But I'm ready to die for Muhammad. I put my bread on the line. I don't have to consult
and come back here at eleven in the morning with my dick
in my hand, permission to piss. I put my bread on the line.
If I got no bread, I'm dead. If I got no loaves, I'm cold
stone in the oven," crooned Bundini. "That's what it's all
about. Muhammad Ali has Bundini ready to die, and what
does the White Man have? Twenty-two niggers and a dog."

Foreman's people roared with all the happiness of knowing that Foreman would win and that the spirit of audacity
was nonetheless not dead. A very heavyset Negro with a
cane for his game leg and heavy horn-rimmed glasses for
his game eyes gave a peal of shrill laughter high as a spurt
of water shooting up, and held out his palm.

Bundini struck it, showed his own palm, the man struck
it back. Happiness. If words were blows, Bundini was
champ of the kingdom of flunkies. Long live Nommo, spirit
of words.

N'GOLO

10. SORCERERS

On Tuesday evening, the night of the fight (which in Kin-shasa would not take place until 4 a.m. on Wednesday morning), something like two hundred journalists were sweating in Press Headquarters at the back of the Hotel Memling. A bureaucratic room offering a dirty floor, dirty beige walls, and rows of aluminum chairs with pale orange plastic bucket seats, it was quickly characterized by the AP man, John Vinocur, as looking like the New York State Employment Office. An inadequate air-conditioning system added its clammy draft to the heat.

Once assembled, the reporters were kept waiting in the Press Room for an hour and a half. From seven in the evening to eight-thirty, two hundred members of the press jammed a room whose fire laws would have closed the door at population eighty, and in the wan light of the fluorescent tubes, reporters were crowded in on one another like a fast-growing culture in a Petri dish. Who knows the murderous remarks of bacteria? The media men talked with passion of Mobutu's lack of faculty for public relations, yet no one dared to leave. The press representative, Tshimpumpu, had announced that he wished to speak to the press. From experience, everyone knew the speech could contain information essential for getting into the stadium, mention of some arcane gate, for example, not listed on the ticket, but crucial. Besides, it was dangerous to miss picking up one's ticket. The rest of the night could be spent pleading with Tshimpumpu's assistants, who would be unable to make a decision without him. God's blood, one didn't want to miss obtaining the ticket now.

Yet as the first half hour went by and then the second, living conditions became intolerable in that overpacked room. After a while one began to recognize there were more important goals in life than fight tickets. Self-preservation might be one of them. An hour in the Press Room of the Memling under these conditions was like a festival for cancer cells. Some boredom was escalation in its promise of future disease.

So Norman Mailer and George Plimpton took off to get a beer and, having found a table in a café across a park behind the Memling (able thereby to keep an eye on the press-room door), were able to relax sufficiently to look for the intent of this peculiar way of distributing seats. Since nothing could have been simpler than to assign an official to a room where he could pass out the tickets as each reporter came by to show his credentials — a modest and natural method used for happier fight promotions — one had here to wonder at the motive: Was it the bureaucratic lust for wanton dislocation on a collective scale, or did Tshimpumpu look to stage the works of Franz Kafka? If the first seemed the likelier explanation, the second finally proved better. For Tshimpumpu never appeared. Murray Goodman, Publicity Director representing the American and English elements of the promotion, Helmdale, Video Techniques, Don King Productions, etc., had the onus of facing the press.

Plimpton and Mailer once safe outside did not know, of course, how wise they had been to leave, but must have sensed it, for they enjoyed the beer, Primus, and the cool African air. They began to talk about Plimpton's luck in finding a fetishist. The day before, Plimpton had mentioned that it might be interesting to visit a conjuror and buy some equivalent of a rabbit's foot on which the sorcerer had worked a magic. "All the rich Blacks in Kinshasa are doing it with their own special medicine men," remarked Plimpton, "and they say it's very expensive. I wonder if you want to come in with me on it."

"We'd buy it for Ali, of course," Norman asked.

"Yes, that's what I thought," said George. His face, however, pinched just perceptibly, a Yankee pinch, that subtle tightening of expression when getting ready to put out a candle with one's fingers. Norman thought he knew what it was. The story could look distasteful in print. They would appear silly if Ali lost, and a hint vainglorious if he won. Besides, Plimpton might wonder how Norman Mailer would handle George Plimpton in the writing.

"On second thought," said George in his fine voice, so reminiscent of the restrained taste for zany leaps and happy improprieties that we used to hear in the voice of Cary Grant, "on second thought, maybe we just ought to ask the *féticheur* to work his magic for a good fight."

"I guess that's reasonable," Mailer said reluctantly.

143

"I think it is," George said.

But now, sitting in the café, he reported a lack of success. The *féticheur* had wanted too much money. "I think what drove the price up," Plimpton confessed, "was his consternation at the demand not to curse one fighter, but give uplift to both. It would have used too much of his stuff."

Later that night, their tickets having put them down side by side in the same press row, Mailer nudged Plimpton right after the huge excitement of the first round. "If we had bought a good fight," he said, "we'd be taking credit now."

That was later. In the beer garden, they had begun to fill in one another on a few stories. There was a studied economy among journalists. To near or equal colleagues, they were willing to give up some large part of their material. If two reporters had the same deadline, they might offer each other nothing (unless it was a question of one losing a job, and even then!) but magazine writers had more time, and ways to live with the same story in separate styles. Often they would give just about all of a good observation away on the knowledge they would get another back. No one was more scrupulous in this regard than Plimpton, and he never failed to provide verbal accounting of an event in his best narrative style so that the work of literature was performed — the story existed for you as he spoke. You could almost live with it as your own perception. And when he did not have a story to offer in return, he might come up with an inspiration to adjust the balance, as he would for instance propose tonight that they travel out together to Nsele and visit Ali just before the fight, an outing which would yet bring them both into Muhammad's dressing room in the thirty minutes before Ali put on his robe and went out to the ring.

On the other hand, you had to give George as much as he gave you. If the account did not run hour to hour, it certainly was kept up more or less day to day. So Mailer, probably feeling himself in arrears by the time they were drinking their beer, went out of his way to give a full account of Foreman's press conference at Nsele the day before. He was, he confessed, getting to like Foreman surprisingly well.

Of course, to speak of liking Foreman was to return to Ogotemmêli's theory of two souls in one body, because Foreman in the ring, working as an executioner, was simply not likable. He might inspire awe at his open desire to demolish an opponent, his sullen reluctance to cease beating on a man once the fight was stopped (so that even the most authoritative referee had to choose a safe moment to come in on Foreman and wave him off) but he would probably win no mass popularity for continuing to hit opponents who were falling to the floor. Nor would anyone forget Foreman's roundhouse shot to the back of Frazier's head as Joe, totally dazed, was staggering away. (It had to be the worst punch seen in a Heavyweight Championship since Ingemar Johansson dropped one of his boulders on the back of Floyd Patterson's neck.) No, Foreman was not likable in the heat of a fight.

In press conferences, however, he was developing considerable charm. He gave them seldom, but he gave them well, and on Monday afternoon after his last workout he talked to the press in his dressing room and was never better. Maybe it was the workout that had put him in so good a mood. It only consisted of a few light rounds with Elmo Henderson but they were conducted in a mood so silent and tender one could have been watching Marcel Marceau. As if to celebrate the intelligence that had gone into his training, Foreman concentrated this last afternoon on the central theme of his work — cut off the ring on Ali, drive him to the ropes, force him to the corner, extinguish him. Elmo was in there playing the part of the flea who went in three, Muhammad Ali, a long thin dying clown, tragic was the face Elmo loaned to Ali in his last extremity, a mournful contemplation of the length of that road which had brought Muhammad here, a sorrow at the depths of his own destruction, yes, Elmo gave a moving imitation of how Ali would seek to employ every feint and guile as he danced around Foreman, but George, faster and faster, happier and happier, would be the master of the ballet. A sweet three rounds. The two men sparred with no heavy punches, just taps of the gloves, and small snaps, scoring on each other to show no more than what they could have done, and Foreman was delighted with Elmo. Both men boxed in the silence of asylum walls, the lack of sound in Henderson's movements as full of presence as the sudden clangor of any *oyé* he would cry on other hours, and Foreman was steeped in the silence, resonant within it. He had never looked more like a boxer.

Afterward in the dressing room, as if in measure to the end of confinement, his good spirits rose. His training was done. He had no more to think about than the fight tomorrow. Never had a fighter looked more relaxed and confident on the day before a fight. As he sat on a rubbing table in the small bare dressing room, he seemed not at all bothered by the twenty-five or thirty reporters who closed around him.

"Are you concerned," one of them asked, "that Ali might be faster than you?"

"It's all a matter of what you call fast," Foreman said. "I don't run 'cause I don't have to. I can hit a man on the jaw fast enough." He relaxed a little more on the laugh that came up on this, and was patient with the next question, which he had heard many times: What did he think of fighting at four in the morning?

This time he gave a different answer. "When I was growing up in Houston, I had a lot of fights at three and four in the morning."

"Were your opponents tough?"

"Right!" He laughed. "I wasn't undefeated then," he said in his mild voice. He shook his head. "I've come a long way from standing on the corner of Lyons Avenue ready to get into something with anybody'd come along. I'd hit 'em and take their cigarettes. That's a long way off from fighting in Kinshasa, Africa" — he corrected himself — "Zaïre, for five million dollars."

"Do you think it'll be a good fight?"

He thought for a while, as if bringing up to date his latest assessment of Ali. "I think it'll be a rightful fight," he replied at last with dignity in his soft voice.

"George, you seem relaxed," a reporter said.

Now he was actually merry. The admiration of the men

questioning him must have been palpable to his flesh. He looked near to sensuous in his calm. "You guys relax me," he said.

"Why?"

"Because you love me," he said (He could sure hit a reporter on the jaw fast enough).

The next question had the harsh and inimitable sense of transition reserved to British reporters. "Of course, Ali doesn't love you," said an English voice. "What do you think of his comment that he's going to tell you something just before the fight begins which is going to affect your mind?"

Foreman shrugged. "I guess he'll have to say it."

"Do you like to speak during a fight?"

"I never do get a chance to talk much in the ring. By the time I begin to know a fellow," George remarked, "it's all over."

That was the interview, short, tasty, no heavy punches, full of confidence. It ended a few minutes later with a conversation on dreams. Already, it has been recorded (by Plimpton in fact) that Foreman recalled a rather complicated dream in which he was teaching a dog how to ice-skate. That dream was a month old and a reporter asked for a new one. Foreman allowed that he sometimes dreamed of eating ice cream cones and woke up with a stomachache. On reflection, one could wonder if that had anything to say about a fear of the world's riches. When it came to emoluments, George had been a modest champion. On the night he defeated Norton, he had been so modest as to get a friend to invite a number of girls up to his suite for a party, and yet he soon retired to another room, where he went to sleep by himself. So it had been reported.

But talk of dreams seemed to irritate Dick Sadler. Near to forty years of managing fighters told him there was nothing good about eating ice cream cones and waking up sick. So he terminated the interview. "George," he said, "I didn't know how big a man you was until they started to ask about your dreams."

Never had the confidence of Foreman's camp seemed stronger than on Monday night. Jim Brown, scheduled to do some of the TV commentary, had arrived in town, Jim Brown the sternest living legend of professional football and he looked like what he had been, a professional gladiator. On this night, thirty hours before the fight, Jim Brown was all out for Foreman's chances, all man about it and no charm. Hard, implacable, and humorless as he described the oncoming fight — correction: possessed of a hard close-out humor. "If Ali wins the fight," he whispers in your ear, "it's been fixed."

For any supporter of Ali, Brown was hard to be with. Yet like all heroes he was magnetic and you hung in to hear his words. Out of his dark steely presence came one full clean force, the clear force of his own knowledge — what Brown knew, he knew. No one else had been able to acquire that knowledge in the way he had, and so one was obliged to listen and weigh his confidence, and try to discount it with the thought that Jim Brown could be in the direct grip of jealousy. If not for Ali, Jim had to be the most important Black athlete in America.

There were other voices to hear that night in the lobby of the Inter-Continental, Marcellus Clay for one, Muhammad's father, but indeed by his features he could have been as easily the father of Jim Brown for he looked to have Indian blood, and took to drink like firewater. One quality the son shared however with the father — nobody was going to lick them — Clay, Senior, ready to drink with anybody, there to curse and bet, wink at anybody — better be female — was popular with the press, although it was hard to capture his dialogue for he had a fast Louisville patter full of slurred sounds and intricate pieces of *talk*, steeped was he in a Southern Black culture of sign painters, barbers, bootblacks, short-order cooks. The press nonetheless loved what they could catch of his sardonic, whining, leaping, snuffling, feisty, rumbling, stumbling, salty, in-and-out whiskey talk. "They's more good-looking womens in Louisville than's showing forth here." Clay, Senior, existed long before Cassius Clay, a classic father of a pugilist — maybe the son can't fight, but the old man sure can!

At the other end of the lobby was Mrs. Clay, who had given Muhammad her good looks, and she was chatting now with Dick Sadler, the two engaged in the most enjoyable conversation and who could guess what it was about? It took all of the good manners one had left to fight down the journalistic lust to eavesdrop on Mrs. Clay and Dick Sadler.

Joe Frazier in an elevator taking notes with Big Black on the problem of getting a good fit for the shoulders when buying a jacket. Frazier is all-out for Foreman. It is possible Joe Frazier will never forgive Muhammad Ali for calling him ignorant.

John Daly: In the lobby, Daly, who brought the first big money to Don King's promotion, $2,000,000 from Helmdale Leisure Corporation. He is a young man, with a bright and happy London face, small, rugged and good-looking, as cheerful as a happy jockey or successful soccer player, and his father is visiting the Inter-Continental now, Tom Daly, a *veteran* British boxer was something like three hundred fights to his record, a small intelligent man who presents a nose with a number of hammered angles and a little damage to his ears, but nothing to his mind, a fine gentleman, Tom Daly, who speaks with respect of Muhammad Ali although he shakes his head, "Does everything wrong and gets away with it." Tom Daly runs a boxing school in London and speaks of fighters as craftsmen or laborers, and lets you in on the rueful situation that all his young hopefuls try to imitate Ali. "Can't be done," he exclaims, "they don't even have the fundamentals."

Bundini: He is telling the crowd, "Today I went to the Black House. Today I met the man and kissed him on the cheek. You got the White House, but I got the Black House."

At dinner: After all this mirth in the lobby, Clarence Jones, a bright well-equipped Black lawyer from New York, is full of the horrendous news that Leroy Jackson, Foreman's lawyer, is now in London attempting to get an extra $500,000 for the fight, and claims Foreman will not appear in the ring until he is given the bonus. It seems much of his $5,000,000 is already attached —·he feels there is nothing left for himself. If Foreman fails to appear in the ring, boxing is not going to recover in a hurry.

"Do you think he'll get it?"

"I'll never speak to John Daly again if he gives another dollar to him," Clarence Jones says in pain. "Foreman is the Champ. He shouldn't act that way."

Now on the following night, after the fight tickets have been safely acquired, Plimpton and Mailer are still talking about the incredible and ugly timing of Foreman's demands. The conversation takes up a good part of the long drive to Nsele, a long forty miles after the number of times they have driven it. The lights of the stadium are lit, however, as they pass; the fight night is here. They ruminate on the peculiarity of Foreman's good mood at his press conference the afternoon before. Were those good spirits rising at the thought of a half-million-dollar gouge? Plimpton talks of how Daly is reputed to be handling it. "I gather he's talking of contracts for future fights. Before long, it'll be time to go into the ring, and too late for Foreman. They say Daly is a master at that." Yet what a peculiar tension for a fighter to put on himself the night of a big bout. Can it do Foreman any good to wonder whether his demand is only a bluff that will be called minute by minute as he gets ready for the ring? It is not only an ugly maneuver, but a foolish one, and makes one begin to wonder at Foreman's confidence. Why would a man who expects to be Champion after this fight look for such an advantage? Yes, there must be two souls in Foreman's body and one of them is not so visible in press conferences. They drive in the African night on the long deserted four-lane road to Nsele — a night of history for Zaïre — but the road is as empty as one's sense of how the fight is going to turn out.

11. A BUS RIDE

BEFORE THE DRIVE, they stopped, however at Kin's Casino, and there each man lost a little at Black Jack. That was about the way Norman wanted it. He was feeling empty — the hour in the Press Room of the Memling had been no good for n'golo. To lose, therefore, was a confirmation of his views on the relation of vital force to gambling. Feeling low in luck, he would just as soon squander this bad luck at the Casino as visit it on Ali. There had been a temptation these last few days to take another walk around the partition on the balcony, only this time do it sober. He had resolutely refused to get into the stunt again, but knew the price: the sense of force within himself would diminish. He even felt a bit of shame at rooting for Ali if he was not ready to take this small dare with himself.

Muhammad was still sleeping when they arrived, or at least was not available to visitors. So they dropped in on Angelo Dundee at his villa and sat there for a while in the quiet boredom of men who were obliging themselves not to feel tension too early. Dundee was the perfect host for such sentiments. He had been living for six weeks in the kuntu of boredom. A wise man from Miami, the banks of the Zaïre were not for Angelo. "I got so bored," he said once to Bud Collins, of the *Boston Globe,* "I was teaching the lizards push-ups." Considered one of the smartest men in boxing, he had managed a number of champions; Carmen Basilio, Willie Pastrano, Jimmy Ellis, Luis Rodriquez, and Ralph Dupas came immediately to mind, and a formidable slew of contenders and TV main-eventers like Mike De John and Florentino Fernandez. Yet Dundee was not Ali's manager, more a glorified trainer. His relation to Ali, while long-standing and professionally intimate, could hardly be called authoritative. Ali would listen to him, but critically. Ali had been in charge of his own training for years. To Dundee, working for Ali was lucrative but could hardly prove satisfying. He was used to taking charge of a fighter. It had been more in his line to work with good fighters and get the most out of them. So, for example, had he schooled Jimmy Ellis on how to back up when fighting Jerry Quarry. "They won't like it," Dundee warned Ellis the night before. "They'll boo you. But you'll win the fight." Dundee had won many a fight like that, and saved many. For one fight, he was famous. There was the legendary moment when Dundee got Cassius Clay back into the ring at the beginning of the fifth round of the first Championship fight with Liston. Clay had been blinded at the time. As afterward reconstructed, the caustic congealing a cut over one of Liston's eyes stuck to Clay's gloves, and between rounds was wiped by accident into his own eyes. Since he could not see, Cassius had a natural reluctance to go out for the fifth round and take the chance of discovering a vision in the light of Liston's punches. Dundee, however, was thinking of higher matters. Reputed to have friendly connections — how could an Italian manager working out of Miami not have such repute? — there would be screams if Cassius Clay refused to come out for the round when ahead on points, double screams when the world learned that Dundee had just been washing his face and the fighter couldn't see. So, at the bell, Angelo pushed him into the ring. Wonders in the ring. Cassius got through the round. Then he went on to win the Championship in another round. His genius for recovery had been disclosed for the first time. What a setback it could have been to his career if Dundee allowed him to stay in the corner. Angelo had been with him ever since.

Now, Dundee was in an armchair watching the television set, and there was nothing on but a three-month-old interview of Ali. Dundee watched it with the animation he would give to an empty screen. A small man with dark hair, olive skin and silver-rimmed eyeglasses, Angelo's exterior was modest. He could pass for an Italian businessman — he offered Sicilian concentricity; himself in the first circle, family in the second, friends and associates in the third.

Sitting with him was Ferdie Pacheco, Ali's doctor, a pleasant-looking man with a meaty face and a New Orleans accent. He was never particularly happy with Ali's condition. A powerful pessimist, he obliged himself when facing reporters to speak like an optimist, but was last known to be confident about a fight the night Jimmy Ellis fought Joe Frazier to settle the Heavyweight title between the World Boxing Association and the New York State Boxing Commission. Frazier was a 4–1 favorite, but Pacheco did not see how Ellis could lose. Frazier knocked out Ellis in five rounds. Pacheco's natural pessimism had been allowed its space ever since. Now, he was also watching television. The TV screen looked like the definitive mandala of monotony. Sitting with them was a small old Black man, an old fight trainer perhaps, with huge somewhat arthritic knuckles. The skin of those knuckles was exceptionally scaly, and he was peeling at the back of his hands. Morose was the mood. You could think the fight had already taken place and Ali lost and they had returned to this villa empty of promise. They looked about as happy as Patterson did coming into the ring for his second fight with Liston.

"Where is Bundini?" Norman asked.

"The star," Angelo answered, "will make his grand entrance in the dressing room. The rest of us will go by bus." It was impossible to tell if this was an old feud, or Dundee's fury was local. Bundini, after all, can live in the Inter-Continental while Angelo is stuck in the mass phallic rectitude of Mobutu.

As good reporters, they inquired of Angelo how Ali had spent his day and were surprised at the news that he jogged out to the pagoda at three-thirty in the afternoon. Was it restlessness? Then he ate, slept, and spent time writing his name on fight tickets being given to friends and guests. Later he watched a movie: Joseph Cotten in *Baron Blood,* a horror film.

"Did he enjoy it?"

"He said he did. He seemed to."

How did Dundee spend his day?

"I was fixing the ring. It was in terrible shape. They didn't have enough resin, and we also firmed up the ring posts. Bob Goodman and I even had to put shims under the floor to tighten the canvas."

One could interpret such details. A tight canvas would be good for Ali's footwork. Dundee was famous for collecting small advantages. Whether he was born with the philosophy or acquired it, his faith was that no advantage could prove too small to take. He even changed a new reporter's money at the official rate of fifty Zaïres for one hundred dollars, when you could get up to eighty on the black market. It was a philosophy that could apply itself to ring posts and resins.

At two in the morning, word came that Ali was ready to leave for the stadium. Plimpton and Mailer got up with the others and walked out to the bus. A small caravan was being set up. Something like five cars and two buses were going to travel in convoy to the stadium. Ali, dressed in a dark shirt and dark pants, was striding about on the grass looking first at one vehicle and then another. He was deciding which one to ride. For a moment he entered the bus, then jumped out again, went to a black Citroën, which he got into with his brother Rachman. He looked nicely keyed up, ready at last for the fight. His careful study of each vehicle did not seem odd to Norman, who had long had the idea that some vehicles promise more luck than others. What is Bantu philosophy ready to say if not that? Luck is the first kuntu.

The convoy set out and proceeded only half a mile. Then it stopped. Word came back along the line. Ali had forgotten his robe. So the vehicles waited at the exit from the press compound of Nsele until the robe was picked up, then set out again.

Mailer and Plimpton were riding in the big bus with Dundee and ten or twelve other people. Few sat together. The loneliness of Ali's camp was evident again. So many of his people were white or pale black. It was the continuing irony of his career. In contrast to Foreman's camp, where Dick Sadler was Black, Sandy Saddler was Black, Henry Clark was Black, Elmo was Black, where the marrow of the mood was Black, Bundini had to be the blackest man in Ali's camp and he was a converted Jew and not even on the bus, and a space existed on the bus between each member of Ali's entourage — how could that not be? Ali's friends and assistants were spokes and Ali was the hub. Take away the hub, and you had a rim with loosened spokes.

There was fear of the fight to come. The mood of the bus was like a forest road on a wet winter day. Only one person seemed cheerful, Aunt Coretta, Ali's cook, whom he had brought from Deer Lake to Nsele. Taking care of his stomach she had the keys to his confidence. She was a big woman, who could have been sister to Ali's mother for they looked something alike, but she was in fact his father's sister, and in her finery tonight, and proud and more than conspicuously careful of her hair, which had been straightened and marcelled and worked upon by an artist who must have been the equivalent of a high pastry chef, yes, there had been collaboration between subject and artist for Aunt Coretta's hairdo, and she had exactly that sense of the worth of her own physical bulk which big hardworking Negro women invariably present when they are dressed and on their way to a special evening. She worked hard enough to enjoy a good time when she had a good time, her life on occasion must be as simple as that, and she was looking forward to the fight. She was confident.

Ali's wife, Belinda, sat at the front of the bus. In Muslim dress with a skirt that came to her ankles, and a white cloth turban close to her head, she was a *statuesque* woman — precisely the word. Over six feet tall, as well proportioned as her husband, she had features sufficiently classic for the head of a Greek statue. In fact if these features were not one chiseled touch smaller than Ali's she could have been his sister in appearance or, better, his female surrogate. They would not have to live together for forty years to look alike. She was also a black belt in karate. She was also shy with strangers. She had the stiffness Black Muslims exhibit in the company of whites. During the trip she spoke only once to the bus at large. "There is," she said, "an ESP psychiatrist in Vegas who said Foreman is going to win. He's going to be psyched tonight." A pause followed in which she may have heard the uncertainty of the silence for she added, "I hope." Yes, that was the mood: hollow, I am nonetheless here to hope.

Of course, Belinda had just returned to Zaïre. She had arrived with Ali six weeks before, but after the postponement she flew back to America. If Ali had a training problem, it was not hard to find. Ever since Joe Namath spent a night with a girl and then went out next afternoon to beat

159

the Baltimore Colts in the Superbowl, next proceeded to tell the world about The Method, the training world of an athlete had been tickled to its root. The impact on sports of Namath's feat was equal to the shock on Henry Luce's American Century when *Sputnik* went up. Every athlete was up against the old question — could the refinement of your best reflexes which sex offered be worth the absence of rapacity it might also leave? At the beginning of his career Ali trained so virtuously that before the time of the first Liston fight, Sonny's people tried to suggest he had never known a woman.

That may have changed. Before the first fight with Frazier, Ali could hardly wait for training to conclude each day — he was known to replace Fiesta or Royal Crown Cola with champagne for supper. Before the first engagement with Norton he was up all night. Doubtless he calculated to sleep all day. Next night, finding himself in the ring, jaw broken, reflexes missing their synapses, he succeeded in dancing his hardworking way through the stupor. He looked awful, he aged that night, but considering his shape, some would argue it was Ali's greatest fight. Days later, jaw wired, orange juice coming through a straw, he must have determined on changing his routine. Training had been less enjoyable since. Nonetheless, Ali's methods remained Ali's own. Belinda had just come back.

Weeks before, boasting to friends in Kinshasa on how he would beat Foreman, Ali said, "He's going to fall on his ass."

"You," Belinda murmured, "better take lessons on how to fall on your ass."

"What did you say?" said Ali.

"I said you better take lessons on how to fall on *your* ass."

"Oh," said Ali, "I thought you said 'fall in love.' "

Led by the blue blinking light of a police car, the convoy continued, but at a slow frustrating pace. Used to going at eighty miles an hour on that stretch of deserted super-highway between Nsele and the airport, they moved along now at half the rate. The empty landscape offered few dis-tractions in the dark. Occasionally, they would pass a few Blacks who were ready to demonstrate at the sight of the convoy, but speed was slow and the mood was slow.

Even as they passed the airport and entered the far out-skirts of Kinshasa, there were still not many people. It was getting near to three in the morning. Whoever was up for the fight had gone to the stadium hours ago. So there was time to meditate on one's own relation to the fight, time to think over the peculiarities of a passion for boxing which could take a man away from his own work for months and more. He even wondered at his loyalty to Ali. A victory for Ali would also be a triumph for Islam. While Norman was hardly a Zionist, and had never gone to Israel, he had been to Cairo and the collision of overflowing new wealth with scabrous poverty, teeming inefficiency, frantic traffic and cripples walking on sores, left him sympathetic to Israel's case. Countries as gargantuan, fascinating, and godawful as Egypt did not deserve to dictate terms to one beleaguered Hebrew idea in the desert. Since he knew little of the pol-itics of the Near East, his politics were as straightforward as that. And conflicted with his loyalty to Ali. Of course he would not be alone in such paradox. It was striking how many of the Jewish writers at Nsele had affection for Ali, a veritable tropism of affection, as if, ultimately, he was one of them, a Jew in the sense of being his own creation. Few things would inspire more love among Jews than the genius to be without comparison.

That could account for much. It could certainly explain why he liked Foreman, and yet was not bothered for an instant in his loyalties. It was as if contradictions fell away with a victory for Ali. That would be a triumph for everything which did not fit into the computer: for audacity, inventiveness, even art. If ever a fighter had been able to demonstrate that boxing was a twentieth century art, it must be Ali. It would certainly come off as a triumph for the powers of regeneration in an artist. What could be of more importance to Norman? He knew some part of him would have to hate Ali if the fighter lost without dignity or real effort, even as a part of him could not forgive Hemingway because of the ambiguity of his suicide — if only there had been a note. The absence of a note left a void in anyone who loved the work and the man.

Yet he in his turn had refused to go out on that balcony without a railing and slip cold sober around the partition. But then he was weary of his comic relation to magic. He never knew which forces he helped. Too many of the fighters for whom he rooted over the years had lost, and lost in miserable encounters. Patterson had lost, for example, in his two fights with Liston, and Sonny lost in his two fights with Ali. Norman had even come to decide that if he was one of a hundred or a thousand magical forces at ringside, his effects were perverse. Or inept. Or scandalously restricted. On the night José Torres beat Willie Pastrano for the Light-Heavyweight Championship, he had been afraid to cheer for fear bad luck would fall upon his friend José. He loved Torres more after the fight because he had been able to win despite the luxury of a friend who was such bad luck as Norman Mailer. That is a frightful idea for a man to have of himself. It is inverse vanity more poisonous than vanity itself. The agent of bad luck. He even doubted whether he had had the right to run with Ali. So a victory for Muhammad on this night would be like a sign of liberation for himself, an indication that he might be rid of the curse of carrying treacherous luck.

They had come to the stadium. It was equal to arriving in the retinue of a matador. The crowds outside were cheering, and police took them through the narrow gates. In less than a minute, the men who had traveled in convoy were in Ali's dressing room. Having said good-bye to Belinda, and given a farewell kiss, the fighter began to get ready.

12. THE DRESSING ROOM

IT WAS a grim dressing room. Perhaps it looked like a comfort station in a Moscow subway. Big, with round pillars tiled in white, even the wallpaper was white. So it also looked like an operating room. In this morgue all groans were damped. White tile was everywhere. What a place to get ready!

The men gathered had no more cheer than the decor. Dundee, Pacheco, Plimpton, Mailer, Walter Youngblood, Pat Patterson, Howard Bingham, Ali's brother Rachman, his manager, Herbert Muhammad, his business manager, Gene Kilroy, Bundini, a small fat Turk named Hassan, and Roy Williams, his sparring partner, were in the room and no one had anything to say. "What's going on here," said Ali as he entered. "Why is everybody so scared? What's the matter with you." He began to peel off his clothes, and wearing no more than a jockstrap was soon prancing around the room, shadowboxing with the air.

Roy Williams, dressed to go into the ring for his semi-final fight with Henry Clark, was sitting on the rubbing table. Through a miscalculation of others, he had arrived at the stadium with the convoy, too late for a ten-round semifinal. They were planning to hold it now after the main event, not the easiest delay for a fighter.

"Scared, Roy?" Ali asked as he danced by him.

"Not a drop," answered Williams in a rich and quiet voice. He was the blackest man in the room, also the gentlest.

"We're going to dance," cried Ali as he flew around, enjoying each near collision with the pillars at his back. Like a child, he had a sense of objects behind him as if the circle of his sensations did not end at his skin. "Ah, yes," he shouted out, "we're going to stick him," and he threw jabs at the air.

With the exception of Roy Williams, he was the only cheerful presence. "I think I'm more scared than you are," said Norman as Ali came to rest.

"Nothing to be scared about," said the fighter. "It's just another day in the dramatic life of Muhammad Ali. Just one more workout in the gym to me." He turned to Plimpton and added, "I'm afraid of horror films and thunderstorms. Jet planes shake me up. But there is no need to be afraid of anything you can control with your skill. That is why Allah is the only One who terrifies me. Allah is the only One of whom the meeting is independent of your will. He is One, and has no associates." Ali's voice was building in volume and piety. As though to protect himself against too much strength being discharged into a sermon, he went on quietly, "There's nothing to be scared of. Elijah Muhammad has been through things that make this night nothing. And in a small way, I have been through such things. Getting

into the ring with Liston the first time beats anything
George Foreman ever had to do, or I have had to do again.
Except for living with threats against my life after the death
of Malcolm X. Real death threats. No, I have no fear of
tonight." He darted away from the writers as if his minute
in the corner was up and shadowboxed some more, teasing
a few friends with quick lancing shots that once more
stopped an inch from their eyes. As he went by Hassan, the
fat little Turk, he extended his long thumb and long forefinger to pinch him in the ass.

Yet for all this fine effort, the mood of the room hardly
improved. It was like a corner in a hospital where relatives
wait for word of the operation. Now Ali stopped dancing
and took out the robe he would wear into the ring and put
it on. It was a long white silk robe with an intricate black
pattern, and his first comment was, "It's a real African robe."
He said this to Bundini, who gave him the full look of a
child just denied a reward which has been promised for a
week.

"All right," Ali said at last. "Let's see your robe."

Now Bundini displayed the garment which he had
brought for Ali to wear. It was also white but had green,
red and black piping along its edges, the national colors of
Zaïre. A green, red, and black map of the country was
stitched over the heart. Bundini wore a white jacket of the
same material and decoration. Ali tried on Bundini's robe,
looked in the mirror, took it off, handed it back. He put on
the first robe again. "This one's more beautiful," he said.
"It's really prettier than the one you brought. Take a look in
the mirror, Drew, it's really better." It was. Bundini's robe
looked a suspicion shopworn.

But Bundini did not look in the mirror. Instead he fixed his look on Ali. He glared at him. For a full minute they scalded one another's eyes. *Look!* said Bundini's expression, *don't mess with the wisdom of your man. I brought a robe which matches my jacket. Your strength and my strength are linked. Weaken me, and you weaken yourself. Wear the colors I have chosen.* Something of that strength had to be in his eyes. Some unspoken threat as well, doubtless, for Ali suddenly slapped him, sharp as the crack of a rifle. "Don't you ever dare do that again," he cried out at Bundini. "Now take a look at me in the mirror," Ali commanded. But Bundini refused to look. Ali slapped him again.

The second slap was so ritual that one had to wonder if something like this was a well-worked ceremony, even an exorcism. It was hard to tell. Bundini seemed too furious to speak. His expression clearly said: *Beat me to death, but I will not look in the mirror. The robe you describe as beautiful is not the one.* Ali finally walked away from him.

It was time to decide on the trunks. He tried several. One pair was all white with no decoration at all, as pure and silver a white as the priestly robes of Islam. "Take this one, Ali," his brother Rachman cried, "take this white one, it's nice, Ali, take it." But Ali after much deliberation before the mirror decided to wear white trunks with a vertical black stripe (and indeed in the photographs one would see later of the fight, there is the black stripe articulating each movement from his torso down to his legs).

Now Ali sat on a rubbing table near the middle of the room, and put on his long white boxing shoes and held each foot in the air while Dundee scraped the soles with a knife to roughen them. The fighter took a comb someone handed him, the Y-shaped comb with steel teeth that Blacks use for an Afro, and worked with deliberation on his hair while his shoes were being scraped. At a signal of his finger, somebody brought him a magazine, a Zaïre periodical in French which gave the complete list of Foreman's fights and Ali's. He read the names aloud to Plimpton and Mailer, and once again contrasted the number of nobodies Foreman had fought with the number of notables he had met. It was as if he had to take still one more look at the marrow of his life. For the first time in all these months, he seemed to want to offer a public showing of the fear which must come to him in a dream. He began to chatter as though no one were in the room and he were talking in his sleep, "Float like a butterfly, sting like a bee, you can't hit what you can't see," he repeated several times as though the words were long gone, and then he murmured, "I been up and I been down. You know, I been around." He shook his head. "It must be dark when you get knocked out," he said, contemplating the ogre of midnight. "Why, I never been knocked out," he said. "I been knocked down, but never *out*." Like a dreamer awakening to the knowledge that the dream is only a net above one's death, he cried out, "That's *strange* . . . being stopped." Again, he shook his head. "Yeah," he said, "that's a bad feeling waiting for night to choke up on you," and he looked at the two writers with the blank eyes of a patient who has encountered some reality in the coils of his condition no doctor will ever comprehend.

Then he must have come to the end of this confrontation with feelings that moved in on him like fog, for he used a phrase he had not employed in months, not since he had last given great woe to every high official in Zaïre, "Yes," he said to the room at large, "let's get ready for the rumble in the jungle," and he began to call to people across the room.

"Hey, Bundini," he cried out, "are we gonna dance?"

But Bundini did not reply. A sorrow was in the room.

"Does anybody hear me?" cried Ali. "Are we going to the dance?"

"We're going to dance and dance," said Gene Kilroy sadly.

"We're going to dance," said Ali, "We're going to da-ance."

Dundee came up to tape his hands. The observer from Foreman's dressing room, Doc Broadus, now moved up to study the operation. He was a short sturdy Black man about sixty who had discovered Foreman years ago in the Job Corps and had been with George for much of his career ever since. Broadus was well known around the Inter-Continental for his prophetic dreams. In his sleep, he had picked the knockout round for both the Frazier and Norton fights. Now for Ali, he had also had a dream that George would win in two rounds, but this time he wasn't making the prediction for certain. There had been some flaw in the dream.

Ali devoted time to talking to him, as if the most valuable man in the room might be Doc Broadus, who could bring back word to Foreman of every detail in his last-minute condition.

Ali stared at him hard, and Broadus shifted his feet. He was shy with Ali. Maybe he had admired his career for too many years to be able to confront him easily now.

"Tell your man," Ali said confidentially, "he better get ready to dance."

Again, Broadus shifted uncomfortably.

At this moment, Ferdie Pacheco came bursting back into the dressing room. He was in a state. "I can't get in to see Foreman," he said to Broadus. "What the hell is going on? What is this?" he said in a tone of fear and considerable shock, "we're boxing tonight, not fighting World War Three!" He seemed disturbed by the fury of the other dressing room. Broadus got up quickly and went out with him.

Now Ali started talking to Bundini. "Say, Bundini, we gonna dance?" he asked. Bundini would not reply.

"I said, are we going to dance?"

Silence.

"Drew, why don't you speak to me?" Ali said in a big voice as if exaggeration were the best means to take Bundini out of his mood. "Bundini, ain't we going to dance?" he asked again, and in a droll tender voice, added, "You know I can't dance without Bundini."

"You turned down my robe," Bundini said in his deepest, huskiest and most emotional voice.

"Oh man," said Ali, "I'm the Champ. You got to allow me to do something on my own. You got to give me the right to pick my robe or how will I ever be Champ again? You going to tell me what to eat? You going to tell me how to go? Bundini, I am blue. I never seen a time like this when *you* don't cheer me up."

Bundini fought it, but a smile began to tickle his lips.

"Bundini, are we going to dance?" asked Ali.

"All night long," said Bundini.

"Yes, we're going to dance," said Ali, "we're going to dance and dance."

Broadus was back from the job of getting Pacheco admitted to Foreman's dressing room, and Ali began to perform for him again. "What are we going to do?" he asked of Bundini and Dundee and Kilroy. "We're going to dance," said Gene Kilroy with a sad loving smile, "we're going to dance all night long."

"Yes, we're going to da-ance," cried Ali, and said again to Broadus, "You tell him to get ready."

"I'm not telling him nothing," muttered Broadus.

"Tell him he better know how to dance."

"He don't dance," Broadus managed to say as if to warn: My man has heavier things to do.

"He don't what?" asked Ali.

"He don't dance," said Broadus.

"George Foreman's man," cried Ali, "says George can't dance. George can't come to the da-ance!"

"Five minutes," somebody yelled out, and Youngblood handed the fighter a bottle of orange juice. Ali took a swig of it, half a glass worth, and stared with amusement at Broadus. "Tell him to hit me in the belly," he said.

13. RIGHT-HAND LEADS

GEORGE WOULD. George was certainly going to hit him in the belly. What a battle was to follow. If the five-minute warning had just been given, it passed in a rush. There was a bathroom off the dressing room and to it Ali retired with his manager, the son of Elijah Muhammad, Herbert Muhammad, a round-faced benign-looking man whose features offered a complete lack of purchase — Herbert Muhammad gave the impression nobody would know how to take advantage of him too quickly. He was now dressed in a priestly white robe which ran from his shoulders to his feet, a costume appropriate to his function as a Moslem minister, for they had gone into the next room to pray and their voices could be heard reciting verses of the Koran — doubtless such Arabic was from the Koran. In the big room, now empty of Ali, everybody looked at everyone and there was nothing to say.

Ferdie Pacheco returned from Foreman's dressing room. "Everything's okay," he stated. "Let's roll." In a minute Ali came out of the bathroom with the son of Elijah Muhammad. While he shadowboxed, his manager continued to pray.

"How are things with Foreman?" someone asked Pacheco, and he shrugged. "Foreman's not talking," he said. "They got him covered with towels."

Now the word came down the line from the stadium outside. "Ali in the ring, Ali in the ring."

Solemnly, Bundini handed Ali the white African robe which the fighter had selected. Then everybody in the dressing room was on their way, a long file of twenty men who pushed and were hustled through a platoon of soldiers standing outside the door and then in a gang's rush in a full company of other soldiers were racing through the gray cement-brick corridors with their long-gone echoes of rifle shots and death. They emerged into open air, into the surrealistic bliss and green air of stadium grass under electric lights, and a cheer of no vast volume went up at the sight of Ali, but then the crowd had been waiting through an empty hour with no semifinal to watch, just an empty ring, and hours gone by before that with dancers to watch, more dancers, then more tribal dancers, a long count of the minutes from midnight to four. The nation of Zaïre had been awaiting this event for three months, now they were here, some sixty thousand, in a great oval of seats far from that ring in the center of the soccer field. They must be disappointed. Watching the fighters would prove kin to sitting in a room in a housing project studying people through a window in another housing project on the other side of a twelve-lane freeway. The fighters would work under a big corrugated tin shed roof with girders to protect the ring and the twenty-five hundred ringside seats from tropical downpour, which might come at any minute on this night so advanced already into the rainy season. Heavy rains were overdue by two weeks and more. Light rain had come almost every afternoon and dark portentous skies hung overhead. In America that would speak of quick summer storms, but the clouds in Africa were patient as the people and a black whirling smoky sky could shift overhead for days before more than a drop would fall.

Something of the weight of this oncoming rain was in the air. The early night had been full of oppression, and it was hot for so early in the morning, eighty degrees and a little more. Thoughts, however, of the oncoming fight left Norman closer to feeling chill. He was sitting next to Plimpton in the second row from the ring, a seat worth traveling thousands of miles to obtain (although counting two round trips, the figure might yet be twenty-five thousand miles — a barrel of jet lag for the soul). In front of them was a row of wire service reporters and photographers leaning on the apron of the ring; inside the ropes was Ali checking the resin against his shoes, and offering flashes of his shuffle to the study of the crowd, whirling away once in a while to throw a kaleidoscope-dozen of punches at the air in two seconds no more — one-Mississippi, two-Mississippi — twelve punches had gone by. Screams from the crowd at the blur of the gloves. He was all alone in the ring, the Challenger on call for the Champion, the Prince waiting for the Pretender, and unlike other fighters who wilt in the long minutes before the titleholder will appear, Ali seemed to be taking royal pleasure in his undisputed possession of the space. He looked unafraid and almost on the edge of happiness, as if the discipline of having carried himself through the two thousand nights of sleeping without his title after it had been taken from him without ever losing a contest — a frustration for a fighter doubtless equal in impact to writing *A Farewell to Arms* and then not being able to publish it — must have been a biblical seven years of trial through which he had come with the crucial part of his honor, his talent, and his desire for greatness still intact, and light came off him at this instant. His body had a shine like the flanks of a thoroughbred. He looked fully ready to fight the strongest meanest man to come along in Heavyweight circles in many years, maybe the worst big man of all, and while the Prince stood alone in his ring, and waited out the minutes for the Champion to arrive and had his thoughts, whatever they were, and his private communion with Allah, however that might feel, while he stood and while he shuffled and while he shadowboxed the air, the Lord Privy Seal, Angelo Dundee from Miami, went methodically from ring post to ring post and there in full view of ringside and the stadium just as methodically loosened each of the four turnbuckles on each post which held the tension of each of the four ropes, and did it with a spoke and a wrench he must have put in his little carrying bag back at Nsele and transported on the bus and carried from the dressing room to this ring. And when the ropes were slack to his taste, loose enough for his fighter to lean way back, he left the ring and returned to the corner. Nobody had paid any particular attention to him.

Foreman was still in his dressing room. Later Plimpton

learned a detail from his old friend Archie Moore. "Just before going out to the ring, Foreman joined hands with his boxing trust — Dick Sadler, Sandy Saddler, and Archie — in a sort of prayer ritual they had practiced (for every fight) since Foreman became Champion in Jamaica," Plimpton wrote. "Now they were holding hands again in Zaïre, and Archie Moore, who had his head bowed, found himself thinking that he should pray for Muhammad Ali's safety. Here's what he said: 'I was praying, and in great sincerity, that George wouldn't *kill* Ali. I really felt that was a possibility.'" So did others.

Foreman arrived in the ring. He was wearing red velvet trunks with a white stripe and a blue waistband. The colors of the American flag girded his middle and his shoes were white. He looked solemn, even sheepish, like a big boy who as Archie said "truly doesn't know his own strength." The letters GF stood out in embossed white cloth from the red velvet of his trunks. GF — Great Fighter.

The Referee, Zack Clayton, Black and much respected in his profession, had been waiting. George had time to reach his corner, shuffle his feet, huddle with the trust, get the soles of his shoes in resin, and the fighters were meeting in the center of the ring to get instructions. It was the time for each man to extort a measure of fear from the other. Liston had done it to all his opponents until he met Ali who, then Cassius Clay at the age of twenty-two, glared back at him with all the imperative of his high-destiny guts. Foreman, in turn, had done it to Frazier and then to Norton. A big look, heavy as death, oppressive as the closing of the door of one's tomb.

To Foreman, Ali now said (as everybody was later informed), "You have heard of me since you were young. You've been following me since you were a little boy. Now, you must meet me, your master!" — words the press could not hear at the time, but Ali's mouth was moving, his head was twelve inches from Foreman's, his eyes were on the other. Foreman blinked, Foreman looked surprised as if he had been impressed just a little more than he expected. He tapped Ali's glove in a move equal to saying, "That's *your* round. Now *we* start."

The fighters went back to their corners. Ali pressed his elbows to his side, closed his eyes and offered a prayer. Foreman turned his back. In the thirty seconds before the fight began, he grasped the ropes in his corner and bent over from the waist so that his big and powerful buttocks were presented to Ali. He flexed in this position so long it took on a kind of derision as though to declare: "My farts to you." He was still in such a pose when the bell rang.

The bell! Through a long unheard sigh of collective release, Ali charged across the ring. He looked as big and determined as Foreman, so he held himself, as if *he* possessed the true threat. They collided without meeting, their bodies still five feet apart. Each veered backward like similar magnetic poles repelling one another forcibly. Then Ali came forward again, Foreman came forward, they circled, they feinted, they moved in an electric ring, and Ali threw the first punch, a tentative left. It came up short. Then he drove a lightning-strong right straight as a pole into the stunned center of Foreman's head, the unmistakable thwomp of a high-powered punch. A cry went up.

Whatever else happened, Foreman had been hit. No opponent had cracked George this hard in years and no sparring partner had dared to.

Foreman charged in rage. Ali compounded the insult. He grabbed the Champion around the neck and pushed his head down, wrestled it down crudely and decisively to show Foreman he was considerably rougher than anybody warned, and relations had commenced. They circled again. They feinted. They started in on one another and drew back. It was as if each held a gun. If one fired and missed, the other was certain to hit. If you threw a punch, and your opponent was ready, your own head would take his punch. What a shock. It is like seizing a high-voltage line. Suddenly you are on the floor.

Ali was not dancing. Rather he was bouncing from side to side looking for an opportunity to attack. So was Foreman. Maybe fifteen seconds went by. Suddenly Ali hit him again. It was again a right hand. Again it was hard. The sound of a bat thunking into a watermelon was heard around the ring. Once more Foreman charged after the blow, and once more Ali took him around the neck with his right arm, then stuck his left glove in Foreman's right armpit. Foreman could not start to swing. It was a nimble part of the advanced course for tying up a fighter. The referee broke the clinch. Again they moved through invisible reaches of attraction and repulsion, darting forward, sliding to the side, cocking their heads, each trying to strike an itch to panic in the other, two big men fast as pumas, charged as tigers — unseen sparks came off their moves. Ali hit him again, straight left, then a straight right. Foreman responded like a bull. He roared forward. A dangerous bull. His gloves were out like horns. No room for Ali to dance to the side, stick him and move, hit him and move. Ali went back, feinted, went back again, was on the ropes. Foreman had cut him off. The fight was thirty seconds old, and Foreman had driven him to the ropes. Ali had not even tried to get around those outstretched gloves so ready to cuff him, rough him, break his grace, no, retreating, Ali collected his toll. He hit Foreman with another left and another right.

Still a wail went up from the crowd. They saw Ali on the ropes. Who had talked of anything but how long Ali could keep away? Now he was trapped, so soon. Yet Foreman was off his aim. Ali's last left and right had checked him. Foreman's punches were not ready and Ali parried, Ali blocked. They clinched. The referee broke it. Ali was off the ropes with ease.

To celebrate, he hit Foreman another straight right. Up and down the press rows, one exclamation was leaping, "He's hitting him with *rights*." Ali had not punched with such authority in seven years. Champions do not hit other champions with right-hand leads. Not in the first round. It is the most difficult and dangerous punch. Difficult to deliver and dangerous to oneself. In nearly all positions, the right hand has longer to travel, a foot more at least than the left. Boxers deal with inches and half-inches. In the time it takes a right hand to travel that extra space, alarms are ringing in the opponent, counterattacks are beginning. He will duck under the right and take off your head with a left. So good fighters do not often lead with their right against another good fighter. Not in the first round. They wait. They keep the right hand. It is one's authority, and ready to punish a left which comes too slowly. One throws one's right over a jab; one can block the left hook with a right forearm and chop back a right in return. Classic maxims of boxing. All fight writers know them. Off these principles they take their interpretation. They are good engineers at Indianapolis but Ali is on his way to the moon. Right-hand leads! My God!

In the next minute, Ali proceeded to hit Foreman with a combination rare as plutonium: a straight right hand followed by a long left hook. Spring-zing! went those punches, bolt to the head, bolt to the head; each time Foreman would rush forward in murderous rage and be caught by the neck and turned. His menace became more impressive each time he was struck. If the punches maddened him, they did not weaken him. Another fighter would be staggering by now. Foreman merely looked more destructive. His hands lost no speed, his hands looked as fast as Ali's (except when he got hit) and his face was developing a murderous appetite. He had not been treated so disrespectfully in years. Lost was genial George of the press conferences. His life was clear. He was going to dismember Ali. As he kept getting hit and grabbed, hit and grabbed, a new fear came over the rows at ringside. Foreman was awesome. Ali had now hit him about fifteen good punches to the head and not been caught once in return. What would happen when Foreman finally hit Ali? No Heavyweight could keep up the speed of these moves, not for fourteen more rounds.

But then the first was not even over. In the last minute, Foreman forced Ali to the ropes, was in on him, broke loose, and smashed a right uppercut through Ali's gloves, then another. The second went like a spear through the top of Ali's skull. His eyes flew up in consternation, and he grabbed Foreman's right arm with his left, squeezed it, clung to it. Foreman, his arm being held, was still in a mood to throw the good right again, and did. Four heavy half-smothered rights, concussive as blows to the heavy bag, went up to the head, then two down to the body, whaling on Ali even as he was held, and it was apparent these punches hurt. Ali came off the ropes in the most determined embrace of his life, both gloves locked around the back of Foreman's neck. The whites of Ali's eyes showed the glaze of a combat soldier who has just seen a dismembered arm go flying across the sky after an explosion. What kind of monster was he encountering?

Foreman threw a wild left. Then a left, a right, a left, a left and a right. Some to the head, some to the body, some got blocked, some missed, one collided with Ali's floating ribs, brutal punches, jarring and imprecise as a collision at slow speed in a truck.

With everybody screaming, Ali now hit Foreman with a right. Foreman hit him back with a left and a right. Now they each landed blows. Everybody was shaking their head at the bell. What a round!

Now the press rows began to ring with comment on those right-hand leads. How does Ali dare? A magnificent round. Norman has few vanities left, but thinks he knows something about boxing. He is ready to serve as engineer on Ali's trip to the moon. For Ali is one artist who does not box by right counter to left hook. He fights the entirety of the other person. He lives in fields of concentration where he can detect the smallest flicker of lack of concentration. Foreman has shown himself a lack of quiver flat to the possibility of a right. Who before this had dared after all to hit Foreman with a right? Of late his opponents were afraid to flick him with a jab. Fast were Foreman's hands, but held a flat spot of complacency before the right. He was not ready for a man to come into the ring unafraid of him. That offered its beauty. But frightening. Ali cannot fight every round like this. Such a pace will kill him in five. Indeed he could be worried as he sits in the corner. It has been his round, but what a force to Foreman's punches. It is true. Foreman hits harder than other fighters. And takes a very good punch. Ali looks thoughtful.

There is a sound box in the vicinity, some small loudspeaker hooked into the closed circuit, and on it Norman can hear David Frost, Jim Brown, and Joe Frazier talking between rounds, an agreeable sense of detachment thereby offered for they are on the other side of the press rows. Listening to them offers the comfort of a man watching a snowstorm from his fireplace. Jim Brown may have said last night that Ali had no chance, but Brown is one athlete who will report what he sees. "Great round for Muhammad Ali," he comments. "He did a fantastic job, although I don't think he can keep up this pace."

Sullenly, Joe Frazier disagrees. "Round was even . . . very close."

David Frost: "You wouldn't call that round for Ali?"

Joe is not there to root Ali home, not after Ali called him ignorant. "It was very close. Ali had two or three good shots to the face while George been landing body shots."

Foreman sits on his stool listening to Sadler. His face is bemused as if he has learned more than he is accustomed to in the last few minutes and the sensation is half agreeable. He has certainly learned that Ali can hit. Already his face shows lumps and welts. Ali is also a better wrestler than any fighter he has faced. Better able to agitate him. He sits back to rest the sore heat of his lungs after the boil of his fury in the last round. He brings himself to smile at someone at ringside. The smile is forced. Across the ring, Ali spits into the bowl held out for him and looks wide awake. His eyes are as alive as a ghetto adolescent walking down a strange turf. Just before the bell, he stands up in his corner and leads a cheer. Ali's arm pumps the air to inspire the crowd, and he makes a point of glowering at Foreman. Abruptly, right after the bell, his mood takes a change.

As Foreman comes out Ali goes back to the ropes, no, lets himself be driven to the corner, the worst place a fighter can be, worst place by all established comprehension of boxing. In the corner you cannot slip to the side, cannot go backward. You must fight your way out. With the screech that comes up from a crowd when one car tries to pass another in a race, Foreman was in to move on Ali, and Ali fought the good rat fight of the corner, his gloves thrown with frantic speed at Foreman's gloves. It became something like a slapping contest — of the variety two tall kids might show when trying to hit the other in the face. It is far from orthodox practice, where you dart out of a corner, duck out of a corner, or blast out. Since Ali kept landing, however, and Foreman did not, George retreated

in confusion as if reverting to memories of fights when he
was ten years old and scared — yes, Ali must have made
some psychological choice and it was well chosen. He got
out of the corner and held Foreman once again by the head
in a grip so well applied that Foreman had the pensive
expression of a steer being dogged to the ground by a
cowboy.

Once the referee separated them, Ali began to back up
across the ring. Foreman was after him throwing fast
punches. "Show him," George's corner must have instructed,
"that your gloves are as fast as his." Suddenly Foreman hit
Ali with a straight hard right. Ali held on to Foreman to
travel through the shock. After the fight he would say that
some of Foreman's punches went right down to his toes, and
this must have been one of them. When the fighters were
separated, Foreman chased Ali to the ropes, and Ali pulled
out a new trick, his full inch and a half of reach. He held
his arms in Foreman's face to keep him off. The round was
almost a minute gone before Ali got in his first good punch,
another right. But Foreman charged him and pushed him,
driving down on Ali's gloves with his own gloves, stalking
him back and back again, knocking Ali's gloves away when
he didn't like the character of their moves. Foreman was
beginning to dictate how the fight should be. If a bully, he
was a master bully. He did not react to the dictation of
others, liked his own dictation. The force he sought in
serenity had locked him on a unilinear road; it was working now. Ali kept retreating and Foreman caught him again.
Hard! Once more, Ali was holding on with both hands,
back of the neck, back of the bicep, half writhing and half

riding with the somewhat stifled punches Foreman kept throwing. Foreman had begun to dominate the action to the point where Ali's best course seemed to be obliged to take what was left of each punch after the attempt to smother it. He kept trying to wrestle Foreman to a stop.

But then Ali must have come to a first assessment of assets and weaknesses, for he made — somewhere in the unremarked middle of the round — he must have made a decision on how to shape the rest of the fight. He did not seem able to hurt Foreman critically with those right-hand leads. Nor was he stronger than Foreman except when wrestling on his neck, and certainly he could not afford any more of those episodes where he held onto Foreman even as George was hitting him. It was costly in points, painful, and won nothing. On the other hand, it was too soon to dance. Too rapid would be the drain on his stamina. So the time had come to see if he could outbox Foreman while lying on the ropes. It had been his option from the beginning and it was the most dangerous option he had. For so long as Foreman had strength, the ropes would prove about as safe as riding a unicycle on a parapet. Still what is genius but balance on the edge of the impossible? Ali introduced his grand theme. He lay back on the ropes in the middle of the second round, and from that position he would work for the rest of the fight, reclining at an angle of ten and twenty degrees from the vertical and sometimes even further, a cramped near-tortured angle from which to box.

Of course Ali had been preparing for just this hour over the last ten years. For ten years he had been practicing to fight powerful sluggers who beat on your belly while you lay on the ropes. So he took up his station with confidence, shoulders parallel to the edge of the ring. In this posture his right would have no more impact than a straight left but he could find himself in position to cover his head with both gloves, and his belly with his elbows, he could rock and sway, lean so far back Foreman must fall on him. Should Foreman pause from the fatigue of throwing punches, Ali could bounce off the ropes and sting him, jolt him, make him look clumsy, mock him, rouse his anger, which might yet wear Foreman out more than anything else. In this position, Ali could even hurt him. A jab hurts if you run into it, and Foreman is always coming in. Still, Ali is in the position of a man bowing and ducking in a doorway while another man comes at him with two clubs. Foreman comes on with his two clubs. In the first exchange he hits Ali about six times while Ali is returning only one blow. Yet the punches to Ali's head seem not to bother him; he is swallowing the impact with his entire body. He is like a spring on the ropes. Blows seem to pass through him as if he is indeed a leaf spring built to take shock. None of his spirit is congested in his joints. Encouraged by the recognition that he can live with these blows, he begins to taunt Foreman. "Can you hit?" he calls out. "You can't hit. You push!" Since his head has been in range of Foreman's gloves, Foreman lunges at him. Back goes Ali's head like the carnival boy ducking baseballs. Wham to you, goes Ali, catapulting back. Bing and sting! Now Foreman is missing and Ali is hitting.

It is becoming a way to fight and even a way to live, but

for Ali's corner it is a terror to watch. In the last thirty seconds of this second round, Ali hits out with straight rights from the ropes fast as jabs. Foreman's head must feel like a rivet under a riveting gun. With just a few seconds left, Foreman throws his biggest punch of the night, an express train of a left hook which leaves a spasm for the night in its passing. It has been a little too slow. Ali lets it go by in the languid unhurried fashion of Archie Moore watching a roundhouse miss his chin by a quarter of an inch. In the void of the effort, Foreman is so off-balance that Ali could throw him through the ropes. "Nothing," says Ali through his mouthpiece. "You have no aim." The bell rings and Foreman looks depressed. There has been premature desperation in that left. Ali shakes his head in derision. Of course that is one of Ali's basic tricks. All through his first fight with Frazier he kept signaling to the crowd that Joe failed to impress him. All the while Ali was finding himself in more trouble.

14. THE MAN IN THE RIGGING

IT SEEMS LIKE eight rounds have passed yet we only finished two. Is it because we are trying to watch with the fighters' sense of time? Before fatigue brings boxers to the boiler rooms of the damned, they live at a height of consciousness and with a sense of detail they encounter nowhere else. In no other place is their intelligence so full, nor their sense of time able to contain so much of itself as in the long internal effort of the ring. Thirty minutes go by like three hours. Let us undertake the chance, then, that our description of the fight may be longer to read than the fight itself. We can assure ourselves: It was even longer for the fighters.

Contemplate them as they sit in their corners between the second and third rounds. The outcome of the fight is not yet determined. Not for either. Ali has an enormous problem equal to his enormous confidence. Everybody has wondered whether Ali can get through the first few rounds and take Foreman's punch. Now the problem has been refined: Can he dismantle Foreman's strength before he uses up his own wit?

Foreman has another problem; he may not be as aware of it as his corner. There is no fear in his mind that he will fail to win the fight. He does not think about that any more than a lion supposes it will be unable to destroy a cheetah; no, it is just a question of catching Ali, a maddening frustration. Still the insult to his rage has to worry his corner. They can hardly tell him not to be angry. It is Foreman's rage after all which has led him to knock out so many fighters. To cut it off is to leave him cowlike. Nonetheless he must contain his anger until he catches Ali. Otherwise he is going to wear himself out.

So Sadler works on him, rubs his breasts and belly, Sadler sends his fingers into all the places where rage has congested, into the meat of the pectorals and the muscle plating beneath Foreman's chest, Sadler's touch has all the wisdom of thirty-five years of Black fingers elucidating comforts for Black flesh, sensual are his fingers as he plucks and shapes and shakes and balms, his silver bracelet shining on his Black wrist. When Sadler feels the fighter is soothed, he begins to speak, and Foreman takes on the expression of a man whose head is working slowly. He has too much to think about. He spits into the bowl held before him and nods respectfully. He looks as if he is listening to his dentist.

In Ali's corner, Dundee, with the quiet concern of a sommelier, is bringing the mouth of the adhesive-taped water bottle to Ali's lips, and does it with a forefinger under the neck so the bottle will not pour too much as he tips it up.

Ali rinses and spits with his eyes off on the serious calculation of a man weighing grim but necessary alternatives.

Joe Frazier: "George is pounding that body with shots.
He's hurting the body. Ali shouldn't stay on that rope. . . .
If he don't move or cut George, George will walk him
down. He need to move. He don't need to stay on that rope.
For what reason's he on the *rope?*" Frazier sounds offended.
Even the sound of the word worries him. Joe Frazier
would consider himself *gone* if he had to work there. Rope
is an ugly and miserable kuntu.

Jim Brown replies: "Ali is punishing George Foreman
even *though* he's on the rope. He's getting some tremendous
blows in and" — the wisdom of the professional football
player — "at some point that can tell."

The bell. Once more Ali comes out of the corner with a
big and threatening face as if this round for certain he will
bring the attack to Foreman and once again sees something
wrong in the idea, profoundly wrong, shifts his plan instantly, backs up and begins to play the ropes. On comes
Foreman. The fight has taken its formal pattern. Ali will go
by choice to the ropes and Foreman will chase him. Now
in each round Ali will work for thirty or forty seconds or
for so much even as a minute with his back no more than
a foot or two from the top rope, and he is on the rope as
often as not. When the strength of the mood, or the logic
of the clinch suggests that the virtue of one set of ropes has
been used up, he will back off across the ring to use another
set. He will spend on an average one-quarter of each round
on each of the four sides of the ring. He might just as well
be drawing conscious strength from the burial gods of the

North, the West, the East and the South. Never has a major fight been so locked into one pattern of movement. It appears designed by a choreographer who knows nothing about the workings of legs and is endlessly inventive about arms. The fight goes on in exactly this fashion round after round, and yet it is hardly boring, for Ali appears in constant danger, and is, and is not. He is turning the pockets of the boxing world inside out. He is demonstrating that what for other fighters is a weakness can be for him a strength. Foreman has been trained to cut instinctively from side to side in such a way as to spoil Ali's ability to circle, Foreman has learned how to force retreat to the ropes. But Ali makes no effort to get away. He does not circle, neither does he reverse his circle. Instead he backs up. Foreman's outstretched arms become a liability. Unable to cuff at a dancing target, he must probe forward. As he does, Ali keeps popping him with straight lefts and rights fast as karate strokes. But then Ali's wife has a black belt in karate.

Sooner or later, however, Foreman is always on him, leaning on him, banging him, belting away with all the fury George knows how to bring to the heavy bag. Ali uses the ropes to absorb the bludgeoning. Standing on one's feet, it is painful to absorb a heavy body punch even when blocked with one's arms. The torso, the legs and the spine take the shock. One has to absorb the brunt of the punch. Leaning on the ropes, however, Ali can pass it along; the ropes will receive the strain. If he cannot catch Foreman's punches with his gloves, or deflect them, or bend Foreman's shoulder to spoil his move, or lean away with his head, slip to the side, or loom up to hug Foreman's head, if finally there is nothing to do but take the punch, then Ali tightens his body and conducts the shock out along the ropes, so that Foreman must feel as if he is beating on a tree trunk which is oscillating against ropes. Foreman's power seems to travel right down the line and rattle the ring posts. It fortifies Ali's sense of relaxation — he has always the last resort of composing himself for the punch. When, occasionally, a blow does hurt, he sticks Foreman back, mean and salty, using his left and right as jabs. Since his shoulders are against the ropes, he jabs as often with his right as his left. With his timing it is a great jab. He has a gift for hitting Foreman as Foreman comes in. That doubles or triples the force. Besides he is using so many right jabs Foreman must start to wonder whether he is fighting a southpaw. Then comes the left jab again. A converted southpaw? It has something of the shift of locus which comes from making love to a brunette when she is wearing a blond wig. Of course, Ali has red wigs too. At the end of the round, Ali hits Foreman with some of the hardest punches of the fight. A right, a left, and a right startle Foreman in their combination. He may not have seen such a combination since his last street fight. Ali gives a look of contempt and they wrestle for a few seconds until the bell. For the few extra seconds it takes Foreman to go to his corner, his legs have the look of a bedridden man who has started on a tour of his room for the first time in a week. He has almost stumbled on the way to his stool.

In the aisle, Rachman Ali began to jeer at Henry Clark. "Your man's a chump," Rachman said. "Ali's going to get him." Clark had to look worried. It was hardly his night.

First his own fight had been postponed, then called off, now he was watching George from a crate in the aisle. Since he had a big bet on George, this last round offered its woes.

In the corner Sadler was massaging Foreman's right shoulder and George was gagging a bit, the inside of his lips showing a shocking frothy white like the mouth of an overgalloped horse.

Nonetheless, he looked lively as he came out for the bell. He came right across the middle of the ring to show Ali a new kind of feint, a long pawing movement of his hands accompanied by short moves of his head. It was to a different rhythm as if to say, "I haven't begun to show what I know."

He looked jaunty, but he was holding his right hand down by the waist. Fatigue must have lent carelessness to what he did, for Ali immediately answered with an insulting stiff right, an accelerating hook and another right so heavy to Foreman's head that he grabbed for a clinch, first time in the fight. There, holding on to Ali while vertigo collided with nausea, and bile scalded his breath, he must have been delivered into a new awareness, for George immediately started to look better. He began to get to Ali on the ropes and hit him occasionally, and for the first time in a while was not getting hit as much himself. He was even beginning to jam a number of Ali's rhythms. Up to now, whenever Ali took a punch, he was certain to come off the ropes and hit Foreman back. A couple of times in this round, however, even as Ali started his move, George would jam his forearm into Ali's neck, or wrestle him to a standstill.

All the while Ali was talking. "Come on, George, show

me something," he would say. "Can't you fight harder? That ain't hard. I thought you was the Champion, I thought you had punches," and Foreman working like a bricklayer running up a pyramid to set his bricks would snort and lance his arms in sudden unexpected directions and try to catch Ali bouncing on the rope, Ali who was becoming more confirmed every minute in the sinecure of the rope, but at the end of the round, Foreman caught him with the best punch he had thrown in many a minute, landing just before the bell, and as he turned to leave Ali, he said clearly, "How's that?"

It must have encouraged him, for in the fifth round he tried to knock Ali out. Even as Ali was becoming more confident on the ropes, Foreman grew convinced he could break Ali's defense. Confidence on both sides makes for war. The round would go down in history as one of the great rounds in Heavyweight boxing; indeed it was so good it forged its own frame as they battled. One could see it outlined forever in lights: *The Great Fifth Round of the Ali-Foreman fight!*

Like much of greatness, the beginnings were unremarked. Foreman ended the fourth round well, but expectation was circling ringside that a monumental upset could be shaping. Even Joe Frazier was admitting that George was "not being calm." It took John Daly to blurt out cheerfully to David Frost, "Ali is winning all the way for me and I think he's going to take it within another four rounds!"

Foreman didn't think so. There had been that sniff of victory in the fourth, the good punch which landed —

"How's that?" He came out in the fifth with the conviction that if force had not prevailed against Ali up to now, more force was the answer, considerably more force than Ali had ever seen. If Foreman's face was battered to lumps and his legs were moving like wheels with a piece chipped out of the rim, if his arms were beginning to sear in the lava of exhaustion and his breath come roaring to his lungs like the blast from a bed of fire, still he was a prodigy of strength, he was *the* prodigy, he could live through states of torture and hurl his cannonade when others could not lift their arms, he had been trained for endurance even more than execution and back in Pendleton when first working for this fight had once boxed fifteen rounds with half a dozen sparring partners coming on in two-round shifts while Foreman was permitted only thirty seconds of rest between each round. He could go, he could go and go, he was tireless in the arms, yes, could knock down a forest, take it down all by himself, and he set out now to chop Ali down.

They sparred inconclusively for the first half-minute. Then the barrage began. With Ali braced on the ropes, as far back on the ropes as a deep-sea fisherman is braced back in his chair when setting the hook on a big strike, so Ali got ready and Foreman came on to blast him out. A shelling reminiscent of artillery battles in World War I began. Neither man moved more than a few feet in the next minute and a half. Across that embattled short space Foreman threw punches in barrages of four and six and eight and nine, heavy maniacal slamming punches, heavy as the boom of oaken doors, bombs to the body, bolts to the head, punching until he could not breathe, backing off to breathe again and come in again, bomb again, blast again, drive and steam and slam the torso in front of him, wreck him in the arms, break through those arms, get to his ribs, dig him out, dig him out, put the dynamite in the earth, lift him, punch him, punch him up to heaven, take him out, stagger him — great earthmover he must have sobbed to himself, kill this mad and bouncing goat.

And Ali, gloves to his head, elbows to his ribs, stood and swayed and was rattled and banged and shaken like a grasshopper at the top of a reed when the wind whips, and the ropes shook and swung like sheets in a storm, and Foreman would lunge with his right at Ali's chin and Ali go flying back out of reach by a half-inch, and half out of the ring, and back in to push at Foreman's elbow and hug his own ribs and sway, and sway just further, and lean back and come forward from the ropes and slide off a punch and fall back into the ropes with all the calm of a man swinging in the rigging. All the while, he used his eyes. They looked like stars, and he feinted Foreman out with his eyes, flashing white eyeballs of panic he did not feel which pulled Foreman through into the trick of lurching after him on a wrong move, Ali darting his expression in one direction while cocking his head in another, then staring at Foreman expression to expression, holding him in the eye, soul to soul, muntu to muntu, hugging his head, peeking through gloves, jamming his armpit, then taunting him on the edge of the ropes, then flying back as Foreman dove forward, tantalizing him, maddening him, looking for all the world as cool as if he were sparring in his bathrobe, now banishing Foreman's head with the turn of a matador sending away a bull after five fine passes were made, and once when he seemed to hesitate just a little too long, teasing Foreman just a little too long, something stirred in George like that across-the-arena knowledge of a bull when it is ready at last to gore the matador rather than the cloth, and like a member of a cuadrilla, somebody in Ali's corner screamed, "Careful! Careful! Careful!" and Ali flew back and just in time for as he bounced on the ropes Foreman threw six of his most powerful left hooks in a row and then a right, it was the center of his fight and the heart of his best charge, a left to the belly, a left to the head, a left to the belly, a left to the head, a left to the belly, another to the belly and Ali blocked them all, elbow for the belly, glove for the head, and the ropes flew like snakes. Ali was ready for the lefts. He was not prepared for the right that followed. Foreman hit him a powerful punch. The ring-bolts screamed. Ali shouted, "Didn't hurt a bit." Was it the best punch he took all night? He had to ride through ten more after that. Foreman kept flashing his muscles up out of that cup of desperation boiling in all determination, punches that came toward the end of what may have been as many as forty or fifty in a minute, any one strong enough to send water from the spine to the knees. Something may have finally begun to go from Foreman's n'golo, some departure of the essence of absolute rage, and Ali reaching over the barrage would give a prod now and again to Foreman's neck like a housewife sticking a toothpick in a cake to see if it is ready. The punches got weaker and weaker, and Ali finally came off the ropes and in the last thirty seconds of the round threw his own punches, twenty at least. Almost all hit. Some of the hardest punches of the night were driven in. Four rights, a left hook and a right came in one stupendous combination. One punch turned Foreman's head through ninety degrees, a right cross of glove and forearm that slammed into the side of the jaw; double contact had to be felt; once from the glove, then from the bare arm, stunning and jarring. Walls must begin to crack inside the brain. Foreman staggered and lurched and glared at Ali and got hit again, zing-bing! two more. When it was all over, Ali caught Foreman by the neck like a big brother chastising an enormous and stupid kid brother, and looked out to someone in the audience, some enemy or was it some spiteful friend who said Foreman would win, for Ali, holding George around the neck, now stuck out one long white-coated tongue. On the other side of the ropes, Bundini was beaming at the bell.

"I really don't believe it," said Jim Brown. "I really don't believe it. I thought he was hurt. I thought his body was hurt. He came back. He hit Foreman with everything. And he winked at *me*." Did he wink or stick out his tongue?

In the aisle, Rachman was screaming at Henry Clark. "Your fighter's a chump. He's an amateur. My brother is killing him. My brother is showing him up!"

15. THE EXECUTIONER'S SONG

So BEGAN the third act of the fight. Not often was there a better end to a second act than Foreman's failure to destroy Ali on the ropes. But the last scenes would present another problem. How was the final curtain to be found? For if Foreman was exhausted, Ali was weary. He had hit Foreman harder than he had ever hit anyone. He had hit him often. Foreman's head must by now be equal to a piece of vulcanized rubber. Conceivably you could beat on him all night and nothing more would happen. There is a threshold to the knockout. When it comes close but is not crossed, then a man can stagger around the ring forever. He has received his terrible message and he is still standing. No more of the same woe can destroy him. He is like the victim in a dreadful marriage which no one knows how to end. So Ali was obliged to produce still one more surprise. If not, the unhappiest threat would present itself as he and Foreman stumbled through the remaining rounds. There is agony to elucidate even a small sense of the aesthetic out of boxing. Wanton waste for an artist like Ali to lose then the perfection of this fight by wandering down a monotonous half hour to a dreary unanimous decision.

A fine ending to the fight would live in legend, but a dull victory, anticlimactic by the end, could leave him in half a legend — overblown in reputation by his friends and contested by his enemies — precisely that state which afflicted most heroes. Ali was fighting to prove other points. So he said. So Ali had to dispose of Foreman in the next few rounds and do it well, a formidable problem. He was like a torero after a great faena who must still face the drear potential of a protracted inept and disappointing kill. Since no pleasure is greater among athletes than to overtake the style of their opponent, Ali would look to steal Foreman's last pride. George was an executioner. Ali would do it better. But how do you execute the executioner?

The problem was revealed in all its sluggish intricacies over the next three rounds. Foreman came out for the sixth looking like an alley cat with chewed-up brows. Lumps and swellings were all over his face, his skin equal to tar that has baked in the sun. When the bell rang, however, he looked dangerous again, no longer a cat, but a bull. He lowered his head and charged across the ring. He was a total demonstration of the power of one idea even when the idea no longer works. And was immediately seized and strangled around the neck by Ali for a few valuable and pacifying seconds until Zack Clayton broke them. Afterward, Foreman moved in to throw more punches. His power, however, seemed gone. The punches were slow and tentative. They did not reach Ali. Foreman was growing glove-shy. His fastest moves were now in a nervous defense that kept knocking Ali's punches away from his own face.

At this point Ali proceeded to bring out the classic left jab everyone had been expecting for the first round. In the next half-minute, he struck Foreman's head with ten head-ringing jabs thrown with all the speed of a good fencer's thrust, and Foreman took them in apathy to compound the existing near-apathy of his hopes. Each time his head snapped back, some communciation between his mind and his nerves must have been reduced. A surgical attack.

Yet something in Foreman's response decided Ali to give it up. Perhaps no more than his own sense of moderation. It might look absurd if he kept jabbing Foreman forever. Besides, Ali needed rest. The next two minutes turned into the slowest two minutes of the fight. Foreman kept pushing Ali to the ropes out of habit, a dogged forward motion that enabled George to rest in his fashion, the only way he still knew, which was to lean on the opponent. Ali was by now so delighted with the advantages of the ropes that he fell back on them like a man returning home in quiet triumph, yes, settled in with the weary pleasure of a working man getting back into bed after a long day to be treated to a little of God's joy by his hardworking wife. He was almost tender with Foreman's laboring advance, holding him softly and kindly by the neck. Then he stung him with right and left karate shots from the shoulder. Foreman was now so arm-weary he could begin a punch only by lurching for-ward until his momentum encouraged a movement of the arm. He looked like a drunk, or rather a somnambulist, in a dance marathon. It would be wise to get him through the kill without ever waking him up. While it ought to be a simple matter to knock him down, there might not be enough violence left in the spirit of this ring to knock him out. So the shock of finding himself on the floor could prove a stimulant. His ego might reappear: once on the floor, he was a champion in dramatic danger of losing his title — that is an unmeasurable source of energy. Ali was now taking in the reactions of Foreman's head the way a bullfighter lines up a bull before going in over the horns for the kill. He bent to his left and, still crouched, passed his body to the right under Foreman's fists, all the while studying George's head and neck and shoulders. Since Foreman charged the move, a fair conclusion was that the bull still had an access of strength too great for the kill.

Nonetheless, Foreman's punches were hardly more than pats. They were sufficiently weak for any man in reasonable shape to absorb them. Still, Foreman came on. Sobbing for breath, leaning, almost limping, in a pat-a-pat of feeble cuffs, he was all but lying over Ali on the ropes. Yet what a problem in the strength of his stubbornness itself. Endless powers of determination had been built out of one season of silence passing into another. The bell rang the end of the sixth. Both men gave an involuntary smile of relief.

Foreman looked ready to float as he came to his corner. Sandy Saddler could not bring himself to look at him. The sorrow in Foreman's corner was now heavier than in Ali's dressing room before the fight.

In his corner Ali looked thoughtful, and stood up abstractedly before the bell and abstractedly led a cheer in the stadium, his arm to the sky.

The cheer stirred Foreman to action. He was out of his corner and in the middle of the ring before the bell rang. Ali opened his eyes wide and stared at him in mock wonder, then in disdain as if to say, "Now you've done it. Now you're asking for it." He came out of his corner too, and the referee was pushing both men apart as the bell rang.

Still it was a slow round, almost as slow as the sixth. Foreman had no speed, and in return Ali boxed no faster than he had to, but kept shifting more rapidly than before from one set of ropes to another. Foreman was proving too sluggish to work with. Once, in the middle of the round, Foreman staggered past Ali, and for the first time in the fight was literally nearer the ropes. It was a startling realization. Not since the first five seconds of the fight had Ali crossed the center of the ring while moving forward. For seven rounds his retreating body had been between Foreman and the ropes except for the intervals when he traveled backward from one set of ropes to another. This time, seeing Foreman on the ropes instead, Ali backed up immediately and Foreman slogged after him like an infantryman looking at the ground. Foreman's best move by now might be to stand in the center of the ring and invite Ali to come to him. If Ali refused, he would lose the luster of his performance, and if he did come forward it would be George's turn to look for weaknesses. While Foreman waited for Ali, he could rest. Yet George must have had some unspoken fear of disaster if he shifted methods. So he would drive, thank you very much, into the grave he would determine for himself. Of course, he was not wholly without hope. He still worked with the idea that one punch could catch Ali.

And with less than a minute left, he managed to drive a left hook into Ali's belly, a blow that indeed made Ali gasp. Then Foreman racked him with a right uppercut strong enough for Ali to hold on in a clinch, no, Foreman was not going to give up. Now he leaned on Ali with one extended arm and tried to whale him with the other. He looked like he was beating a rug. Foreman had begun to show the clumsiness of a street fighter at the end of a long rumble. He was reverting. It happened to all but the most cultivated fighters toward the exhausted end of a long and terrible fight. Slowly they descended from the elegance of their best style down to the knee in the groin and the overhead punch (with a rock in the fist) of forgotten street fights.

Ali, half as tired at least, was not wasting himself. He was still graceful in every move. By the end of the round he was holding Foreman's head tenderly once more in his glove. Foreman was becoming reminiscent of the computer Hal in 2001 as his units were removed one by one, malfunctions were showing and spastic lapses. All the while something of the old panache of Sadler, Saddler, and Moore inserted over those thousands of hours of training still showed in occasional moves and gestures. The weakest slaps of his gloves, however, had begun to look like entreaties. Still his arms threw punches. By the end of the seventh he could hardly stand: yet he must have thrown seventy more punches. So few were able to land. Ali had restricted himself to twenty-five — half at least must have gone to target. Foreman was fighting as slowly as a wornout fighter in the Golden Gloves, slow as a man walking up a hill of pillows, slow as he would have looked if their first round had been rerun in slow motion, that was no slower than Foreman was fighting now, and thus exposed as in a film, he was reminiscent of the slow and curving motions of a linebacker coiling around a runner with his hands and arms in the slow-motion replay — the boxing had shifted from speed and impact to an intimacy of movement. Delicately Ali would cradle Foreman's head with his left before he smashed it with his right. Foreman looked ready to fall over from exhaustion. His face had the soft scrubbed look of a child who has just had a dirty face washed, but then they both had that gentle look boxers get when they are very tired and have fought each other very hard.

Back in the corner, Moore's hands were massaging Foreman's shoulders. Sandy Saddler was working on his legs. Dick Sadler was talking to him.

Jim Brown was saying, "This man, Muhammad Ali, is *unreal.*" When Jim used the word, it was a compliment. Whatever was real, Jim Brown could dominate. And Frazier added his humor, "I would say right now my man is not in the lead. I got a feeling George is not going to make it."

On the aisle, Rachman was still calling out to Henry Clark. "Henry, admit it, your man is through, he's a chump, he's a street fighter. Henry, admit it. Maybe I'm not a fighter, I know I'm not as good as you, but admit it, admit it, Muhammad has whipped George."

Except he hadn't. Not yet. Two rounds had gone by. The two dullest rounds of the fight. The night was hot. Now the air would become more tropical with every round. In his corner, Ali looked to be in pain as he breathed. Was it his kidneys or his ribs? Dundee was talking to him and Ali was shaking his head in disagreement. In contrast to Foreman, his expression was keen. His eyes looked as quick as the eyes, indeed, of a squirrel. The bell rang for the eighth round.

Working slowly, deliberately, backing up still one more time, he hit Foreman carefully, spacing the punches, taking aim, six good punches, lefts and rights. It was as if he had a reserve of good punches, a numbered amount like a soldier in a siege who counts his bullets, and so each punch had to carry a predetermined portion of the work.

Foreman's legs were now hitched into an ungainly prance like a horse high-stepping along a road full of rocks. Stung for the hundredth time with a cruel blow, his response was to hurl back a left hook that proved so wild he almost catapulted through the ropes. Then for an instant, his back and neck were open to Ali, who cocked a punch but did not throw it, as though to demonstrate for an instant to the world that he did not want to flaw this fight with any blow reminiscent of the thuds Foreman had sent to the back of the head of Norton and Roman and Frazier. So Ali posed with that punch, then moved away. Now for the second time in the fight he had found Foreman between himself and the ropes and had done nothing.

Well, George came off the ropes and pursued Ali like a man chasing a cat. The wild punch seemed to have refreshed him by its promise that some of his power was back. If his biggest punches were missing, at least they were big. Once again he might be his own prodigy of strength. Now there were flurries on the ropes which had an echo of the great bombardment in the fifth round. And still Ali taunted him, still the dialogue went on. "Fight hard," said Ali, "I thought you had some punches. You're a weak man. You're all used up." After a while, Foreman's punches were whistling less than his breath. For the eighteenth time Ali's corner was screaming, "Get off the ropes. Knock him out. Take him home!" Foreman had used up the store of force he transported from the seventh to the eighth. He pawed at Ali like an infant six feet tall waving its uncoordinated battle arm.

With twenty seconds left to the round, Ali attacked. By his own measure, by that measure of twenty years of boxing, with the knowledge of all he had learned of what could and could not be done at any instant in the ring, he chose this as the occasion and lying on the ropes, he hit Foreman with a right and left, then came off the ropes to hit him with a left and a right. Into this last right hand he put his glove and his forearm again, a head-stupefying punch that sent Foreman reeling forward. As he went by, Ali hit him on the side of the jaw with a right, and darted away from the ropes in such a way as to put Foreman next to them. For the first time in the entire fight he had cut off the ring on Foreman. Now Ali struck him a combination of punches fast as the punches of the first round, but harder and more consecutive, three capital rights in a row struck Foreman, then a left, and for an instant on Foreman's face appeared the knowledge that he was in danger and must start to look to his last protection. His opponent was attacking, and there were no ropes behind the opponent. What a dislocation: the axes of his existence were reversed! He was the man on the ropes! Then a big projectile exactly the size of a fist in a glove drove into the middle of Foreman's mind, the best punch of the startled night, the blow Ali saved for a career. Foreman's arms flew out to the side like a man with a parachute jumping out of a plane, and in this doubled-over position he tried to wander out to the center of the ring. All the while his eyes were on Ali and he looked up with no anger as if Ali, indeed, was the man he knew best in the world and would see him on his dying day. Vertigo took George Foreman and revolved him. Still bowing from the waist in this uncomprehending position, eyes on Muhammad Ali all the way, he started to tumble and topple and fall even as he did not wish to go down. His mind was held with magnets high as his championship and his body was seeking the ground. He went over like a six-foot sixty-year-old butler who has just heard tragic news, yes, fell over all of a long collapsing two seconds, down came the Champion in sections and Ali revolved with him in a close circle, hand primed to hit him one more time, and never the need, a wholly intimate escort to the floor.

The referee took Ali to a corner. He stood there, he seemed lost in thought. Now he raced his feet in a quick but restrained shuffle as if to apologize for never asking his legs to dance, and looked on while Foreman tried to rouse himself.

Like a drunk hoping to get out of bed to go to work, Foreman rolled over, Foreman started the slow head-agonizing lift of all that foundered bulk God somehow gave him and whether he heard the count or no, was on his feet a fraction after the count of ten and whipped, for when Zack Clayton guided him with a hand at his back, he walked in docile steps to his corner and did not resist. Moore received him. Sadler received him. Later, one learned the conversation.

"Feel all right?"

"Yeah," said Foreman.

"Well, don't worry. It's history now."

"Yeah."

"You're all right," said Sadler, "the rest will take care of itself."

In the ring Ali was seized by Rachman, by Gene Kilroy, by Bundini, by a host of Black friends old, new and very new, who charged up the aisles, leaped on the apron, sprang through the ropes and jumped near to touch him. Norman said to Plimpton in a tone of wonder like a dim parent who realizes suddenly his child is indeed and indubitably married, "My God, he's Champion again!" as if one had trained oneself for years not to expect news so good as that.

In the ring Ali fainted.

It occurred suddenly and without warning and almost no one saw it. Angelo Dundee circling the ropes to shout happy words at reporters was unaware of what had happened. So were all the smiling faces. It was only the eight or ten men immediately around him who knew. Those eight or ten mouths which had just been open in celebration now turned to grimaces of horror. Bundini went from laughing to weeping in five seconds.

Why Ali fainted, nobody might ever know. Whether it

was a warning against excessive pride in years to come —
one private bolt from Allah — or whether the weakness of
sudden exhaustion, who could know? Maybe it was even
the spasm of a reflex he must have refined unconsciously
for months — the ability to recover in seconds from total
oblivion. Had he been obliged to try it out at least once
on this night? He was in any case too much of a champion
to allow an episode to arise, and was back on his feet before ten seconds were up. His handlers having been lifted,
chastened, terrified and uplifted again, looked at him with
faces of triumph and knockdown, the upturned mask of
comedy and the howling mouth of tragedy next to each
other in that instant in the African ring.

David Frost was crying out: "Muhammad Ali has done
it. The great man has done it. This is the most joyous scene
ever seen in the history of boxing. This is an incredible
scene. The place is going wild. Muhammad Ali has won."
And because the announcer before him had picked the
count up late and was two seconds behind the referee and
so counting eight when Clayton said ten, it looked on all
the closed circuit screens of the world as if Foreman had
gotten up before the count was done, and confusion was
everywhere. How could it be other? The media would always sprout the seed of confusion. "Muhammad Ali has
won. By a knockdown," said Frost in good faith. "By a
knockdown."

Back in America everybody was already yelling that the
fight was fixed. Yes. So was *The Night Watch* and *Portrait
of the Artist as a Young Man*.

16. THE RAINS CAME

For reporters, the fight had just begun. They had to get into Ali's dressing room. It became Norman's exclusive, his first. How he got in he was never able to calculate later, but a considerable amount of timely pushing through the squad of soldiers at the door had something to do with it. You had to shove hard enough to make progress, but not so hard that you would promote a rifle butt in your ribs — his final grand effort got one leg through just back of a fat man he had never seen before.

In the dressing room they were trying to slam the door to protect Ali from an inundation of flesh, so there was a minute where Norman was happy for every muscle he had. When someone made a lunge to get in behind him, the vanguard came down to parts of three bodies coming through the door at once. Since he was in the middle, and the other torsos were soft, he was ensconced. What a timeless squeeze.

Pat Patterson, with a chrome-plated pistol on his hip and a cop's rage at the assault on his bastion, finally gave a hand to drive the others out and pull Norman in. To his surprise he was the only reporter in the room. Never did a man proceed to do less with his exclusive. Of course, he would have months to write his piece and half a year to see it printed — there was hardly the need to rush to a telephone in the next ten minutes. But even if a man had been waiting thousands of miles away at a city desk, he might have done no more. He didn't want to ask Ali questions, he wanted to pay his respects. There are not that many occasions in life, after all, when the sense of irony has clearly departed.

Ali sat on the rubbing table with his hands on his knees looking like a happy and tired host after a good party. His face was unmarked except for a small red bruise on one cheekbone. Maybe he never appeared more handsome. He stared out like a child. "I have stolen the jam," said his eyes, "and it tastes good." Light twinkled in those eyes all the way back to the beginning. Truth, he looked like a castle all lit up.

"You did everything you said you were going to do," Norman offered in simple tribute.

"Yeah. It was a good night." Neither mentioned that he had not danced. That must have been the surprise he promised.

"Fantastic fight," Norman said. "You're going to like looking at the films."

Ali drew a breath. "Maybe they'll admit," he said softly, "that now I am the professor of boxing."

The door to the dressing room was opened again to admit Belinda Ali. Husband and wife looked at each other silently as if a question of long standing was at last being resolved. They kissed. The object of love would prove for once deserving of love. He gave her a smile as open as the sweetness of his feelings. There was something so tender in Ali's regard, so mocking, and so calm, that the look appeared to say, "Honey, my ways got to be curious to you, and we both know I am crazy, but please believe me when I try to tell you that I am, my darling, by all scientific evidence a serious fellow." (Or is that the way Norman would have spoken if he had ever won anything that well?)

Belinda now moved around the room to exchange congratulations. She made a point of going up to Roy Williams, who had waited through this long night without a fight. "I want to thank you, Roy, for all you've done," she said. "We couldn't have won this fight if you hadn't gotten Ali ready the way you did."

"Thank you," he said with pleasure, "it was sure a good night."

"I'm sorry you didn't have your fight."

"Oh," said Roy in his deep voice, "Ali won and *that* counts."

If Norman had been keeping his journalistic wits, he would now have gone to the other dressing room, but he wanted to discuss the fight with Ali, a feeble practical judgment. Other reporters were getting in to see the new Champion, and so many surrounded the rubbing table and Ali spoke in so low a voice that no more rations for the literary mill were going to be collected.

By the time he left, Norman would discover to his unhappiness that he had missed George Foreman in his dressing room, a sore loss, for Foreman had things to say. Other reporters filled him in, notably Plimpton and Bob Ottum of *Sports Illustrated*. Given the essential generosity of reporters to one another, it was all too easy to form atrocious habits and cover one's stories from the telephone in the bathtub. Yes, even as reconstructed, Foreman had things to say. Yet what a loss not to feel the battered aura of the ex-Champion's mood. Every wound has its own revelation.

The dressing room he never saw had red walls, and the fighter after the fight was covered with towels in gold lamé. "I got to beat this guy," Ali had said once. "I saw him at Salt Lake City. He was wearing pink and orange shoes with platforms and high heels. I wear brogans. When I saw his fly shoes, I said to myself, 'I'm going to win.'"

Yes, red and gold for fallen kings. Foreman lay beneath ice packs. According to Plimpton he first asked Dick Sadler if he had been knocked out, then he counted backward for a while from a hundred, ninety-nine, ninety-eight, to see if his head was clear, and he called out the names of the twenty people in his camp one by one. "I felt secure," said Foreman. "I had a true feeling I was in control of this fight. I was surprised when the people jumped into the ring." He said everything in a quiet calm voice. "I was counted out," he said, "but I was not knocked out."

Let us quote Plimpton's account here:

He repeated, at times so slowly that it seemed as if he were stumbling through a written text, what he had so often said in dressing-room statements following his victories: "There is never a loser. No fighter should be a winner. Both should be applauded."

The reporters stood around uncomfortably, knowing that it would finally sink in that for the first time in his professional career his generous words for a loser referred to himself.

Then Foreman spoke of Ali. "A fine American," he said, "great gentleman. A wonderful family man." The reporters were counting how many times Foreman had been hit in the head over eight rounds.

He was still talking as the winner. There is all the temporary insanity of loss. One knows that there is a reality to which one can return, at least the odds are great that it will still be there, but reality does not feel real. It is too insubstantial. Reality has become a theory introduced into one's head by other people. It does not seem as natural as what one feels. George Foreman still felt like the Champion.

He took the ice pack off his face. "I have a statement to make. I found true friendship tonight," he said "I found a true friend in Bill Caplan."

That was Bill Caplan who beat Foreman at Ping-Pong every day. Sturdy Bill Caplan with his round face, his eye-glasses, and a hundred reporters always mad at him because Foreman was uncooperative about interviews. With what eyes of Jewish compassion must Caplan have looked at Foreman after the fight. George's own people would not be so kind. By Black measure, defeat is as bad as disease.

"I imagine," said George, "that the punch that knocks a man down he doesn't really see. I suspect he doesn't know about it."

There were crowds on the street outside the stadium, and Blacks celebrating in the dawn. It was as if they had not dared to feel too much hope for Ali in advance of the fight. Yet just as there are men who only reach their rightful historical stature in the hour of assassination, so others do it on the morning of their victory. Outside the stadium, at 6 A.M., there was a crazy air of liberation all over the boulevards and back streets of Kinshasa. People were drunk, people were bowing to one another, people extended their arms and legs in the long moves appropriate to a basketball court. That seemed the way to float down the road. There was laughter, and people waving to one another two blocks away. Catcalls at the sight of him. A white man. Must certainly be for Foreman. Yes, the sweet spirit of revolution was back, not all sweet, let us say it is the spirit of change, and lions, cockroaches, and philosophers are all awake. Nommo (if we remember) is the Word, and the word is in the water, and life is in the air. The damp air on this dawn is full of the n'golo of the living and the thirst of the dead. It is a weird morning. Under these heavy clouds, there is a dawn which does not lift. The light is reminiscent of the pallor of the earth in an eclipse.

On the street, Norman has run into a gambling friend he knows at the Casino and the two debate whether to try to walk all the way home, but it is eight miles and more. Finally they get a cab. His friend promotes it. His friend sees a whore he knows passing in a cab and calls to her and offers to pay the fare if she will share it with them. She is a young and lovely whore with a dark bronze skin, a body as lithe as a climbing vine, and an abundance of dark bronze hair in her armpits. She is at this hour in love with Muhammad Ali — one does not wish to change places with her pimp at this hour. She will not appear again in our account and since Africans, according to good Father Tempels, believe "the name is not a simple external courtesy, it is the very reality of the individual," let us give to print the full value of the reality she chooses for herself — which is Marcelline. They leave her soon at her house, a hovel with a tin roof on a humped dirt road with oil stains, tropical puddles, and dead foliage. Marcelline has been as beautiful as a movie star.

At the Inter-Continental, everybody is drinking in the timeless dawn. At the bar and on the patio people are celebrating, people are toasting the morning in champagne. He runs into Jim Brown and cannot resist asking, "Think the fight was fixed?" Jim Brown grins ruefully, he shakes his head. He is happy to feel in error. "Man," he says, "I never been more wrong in all my life."

One by one, Foreman's people were there to talk to. Maybe it is the mark of a good man that defeat does not leave more than one good sentence in the mouth. Henry Clark, having lost his big bet, merely said, "The better fighter won." Doc Broadus looked sad but firm. "It did him good," was his measure. Foreman's Uncle Hayward, a big old Black man with powerful connections and a huge kettle-drum paunch reminiscent of classic Southern white politicians, replied in answer to the wish that people not call George a bum, "He deserves to be called a bum."

Elmo, encountered in the lobby, was not saying a word. Norman said at last, "George met the man at his best."

Elmo gave a silent nod. He smiled. "Working on it," he said. "*Oyé.*"

Archie Moore let a few words drop: "Boxing is syllables. You learn them one by one." Still his eyes had a light. He was loyal to George, but Ali was the triumph of his own tradition.

Dick Sadler talked at length. If he was a good man, then defeat gives speech to some. "It wasn't what Muhammad did," Sadler said, "it was what George didn't do. He didn't move. He didn't listen. I don't know what was going on. George don't let anybody hold him. He let Muhammad. We told him Muhammad was going to hold. George knew before the fight what Muhammad was going to do. But he punched himself out. George can punch all day. How does he punch himself out? I'm going crazy. Big bad George Foreman, known to be a brutal fighter, hits people back of the head, hits men when they're sitting on the ropes, hits them when they're down, bombs them in the kidney, a rough mean fighter, and he lets Muhammad hold him. I showed him what to do. If Muhammad's got his gloves up protecting his head, then he can't see, so, George, poke him where he's blind. If he's down protecting his gut, let him hear it in the ear. Set him up with the left, George, give it to him with the right. He wouldn't do it, he couldn't do it."

"Maybe Ali is different from other fighters." Norman was tempted to broach his idea that this was the first major fight which bore serious resemblance to chess. Such comparisons were sentimental conceits, and this was hardly the time. Still!

It is fortunate he kept his mouth shut for Sadler next remarked, "I'm just as stupid on the fight as you are. I got to think about it."

A six-year-old girl, down for early breakfast, early as could be, passed by and Sadler went to give her a hug. "*Bonjour, ma petite*," he said, "*Bonjour.*"

The conversation still bothered him, however. He came back to Norman, and said, "I ain't got the answer."

Then the rainy season, two weeks late, and packed with the frenzy of many an African atmosphere and many an unknown tribe, came at last to term with the waters of the cosmos and the groans of the Congo. The rainy season broke, and the stars of the African heaven came down. In the torrent, in that long protracted moon-green dawn, rain fell in silver sheets and silver blankets, waterfalls and rivers, in lakes that dropped like a stone from above, and with a slap of contact louder than the burst of fire in a forest. It came in buckets, a tropical rain right out of the heart overhead. He had not seen a rain so bad in thirty years, not since he sat under a pup tent in the Philippines.

Later he heard what the storm did to the stadium. It poured onto the seats and poured through the aisles, it flowed down in jungle falls and streamed through the stairs and narrow entry halls, flooded the soccer field and washed beneath the ring carrying for its message the food and refuse of the sixty thousand souls once sitting in the seats. Foreman's dressing room was a dark pool with old towels floating in a foot of water, the kids were prowling the stadium by the end of the deluge. Orange peels and fight tickets drifted into collection beneath the canvas, and batteries were drenched, generators gave out. Half the Telex machines broke down in the storm, and the satellite ceased to send a picture or a word. What a debacle if the storm had come while the fight was on.

Ali would laugh next day and offer to take credit for holding back the rain.

17. A NEW ARENA

On that next day (which is the same day just after sleeping from nine to noon) Norman had lunch and decided to go out to Nsele one last time and say good-bye to Ali. On the way, he was thinking of a conversation he might like to have with the fighter, and wondered if it wouldn't be easy when all was said to explain to Ali how the fight was not only a revolution in boxing (with which Ali would certainly agree) but had a counterpart in modern chess.

Since Norman was always too ready to serve as matrimonial agent to the mating of large ideas, and prone to offer weighty metaphors without constructing a seat, he tried these days to be careful. A writer does well to work on his vice. Still, he liked the new idea. In chess, no concept had once been more firmly established than control of the center, and for much the same reason as boxing — it gave mobility for attack to the left or the right. Later, a revolution came to chess, and new masters argued that if one occupied the center too early, weaknesses were created as well as strengths. It was better to invade the center after the opponent was committed. Of course with such a strategy you had to be resourceful in a cramped space. Tactical brilliance was essential at every step. Was that not exactly what Ali had accomplished? It was doubtful, however, if many a chess game had been played which equaled in timing Ali's climactic occupation of the center of the ring.

Having been overpowered in his youth by the works of Karl Marx and Oswald Spengler, Norman used to love Germanic formulation. Years ago, he could have written, "There are profound historic relations between the relinquishment of the center by Nimzovitch and Réti (with their subsequent inspiration upon the schools of Hypermodern and Dynamic chess) and the boxing techniques of the American Heavyweight Muhammad Ali who has introduced to pugilism the modal transposition from Active to Passive demanded by the techno-revolutionary *geist* of the last decades of the Twentieth Century so essential to the liberation of the woman, a reversal of polarity in established structures of power which becomes the technological and/or the mystical signature of the century," yes, his style has improved a little, but we can tell by his love of African philosophy that Norman still believes history is an organism, and reveals a sense of style, a divine stroke of the pen to every era. It is not even hard to describe, but it is difficult to say without being guillotined by the critics (who as a body of clerks seem never to have advanced beyond the simple life-giving love of reason — and taste for fresh blood — of the French Revolution).

Enough! Let us look for Ali. Norman, of course, does not have a conversation about chess with him. They are hardly to be alone. If they were, Ali would have small interest. His mind is attached to his own ideas.

Out there, the new Champion is giving a press conference to a hundred African reporters and media men who gather around him with the solemnity and respect they might once have offered to Gandhi. It is three in the afternoon, not ten hours since he won, and he has probably not slept for half of that time — nonetheless his tongue is unflagging and he must talk on fifty subjects, telling the Third World press in just the short time Norman is there how "the long dresses of your women impress me more than your jet planes and your Lumumba monument." A little later he compliments them on changing their names to African. "On the occasion of his investiture," writes Father Tempels, the chief "receives a (new) name. . . . His former name may be no longer uttered, lest by so doing his new vital force may be harmed." Muhammad Ali, né Cassius Clay, knew whereof he spoke, and talked of the emergence of peoples and the disciplines of victory and the need for goals outside the vanity of the self. "These things George Foreman did not recognize," he intoned. "But I know that beating George Foreman and conquering the world with my fists does not bring freedom to my people. I am well aware that I must go beyond all this and prepare myself for more. I know," said Muhammad Ali, "that I enter a new arena."

My God! All of it! He was going after all of it. And why not, given the rate of increase at which he mastered the whole of whatever he was given. Norman was thinking of the first time he met him, there at a crap table in The Dunes, Cassius Clay in Vegas in the summer of 1963, a tall skinny nervous young fighter with an undefeated record and a mortal fear of Sonny Liston, whom soon he was going to meet. The boy was unhappy with the half-recognition of the name. "Norm Mailer, I heard of you. You're in the movies or something" — the boy did not like to be unsure — and later throwing the dice, so ignorant of craps he hardly knew when he won yet still lucky as the vein of his ongoing fortune, Cassius complained when they passed him casino counters after a winning roll. "What are these things?" he cried.

"Chips."

"Don't gimme none of that stuff," he bawled. "Gimme some more of those silver dollars!" Just another mad-hat lout from Louisville. Now he was entering a new arena. "He who is not courageous enough to take risks will accomplish nothing in life," he told the representatives of the Black media. "That is why I love and respect Africa. It is the land of risks and" — he looked for the word — "endeavor. The people have respect, yet they are brave to new notions. They are the force of the future." With what an immensity of anxiety must Ali live at the size of his world role and his intimate knowledge of his own ignorance.

Later, he and Budd Schulberg were alone with Ali for a few minutes, and started to have a good talk about the fight. Ali was getting ready to expatiate. He was in the full enjoyment of analyzing his own fight. "George, you see," he said, "has got a breathing problem." But they were interrupted. John Daly and a group of his friends had come to visit the villa. Ali, with the happiest spirit, was soon charming the ladies. "Oh," he said in response to a query, "my mother never worries. I could be getting killed in the ring, but she wouldn't worry. 'My baby's all right,' she'd be saying." And he winked at Tom Daly, John Daly's father, with his three hundred fights, to whom he had just been introduced. The phone rang. It was a reporter in New York, and Ali talked to him, and made faces with his guests. "Yes, I will rest a few months and let you look at me as the Champ and him as the tramp." Laughter from the people near him. "No, I have no plans. They're talking of giving me ten million dollars" — a straight look at John Daly — "but that's ahead. No, I have no plans to visit the White House. I'm going to visit the Black House right here, and see the president of Zaïre again and get my pet gorilla, and take my little Joe Frazier home." He waited for the laughter and the next question. "You're asking if I was happy to get the title back in Africa, which is the home of my ancestors? Yes, I was happy, a good feeling, but it don't mean too much. I'd rather have done it in Madison Square Garden because that's where the real nonbelievers are, that's the real fight crowd."

Later, after company left, and evening was falling on the Congo, Ali went out for a short walk, but was followed by so many Black people waiting outside the villa for a look at him that he soon came back. The red bruise on his cheek had subsided and his face was unmarked. The only sign he had been in a fight is that he moved with an extra subtlety of anticipation like a man who has been in a wreck and does not know where pains will yet disclose themselves. He has taken a pounding to the side of his body and the top of his kidneys. In the privacy of his bathroom, doubtless he will wince and piss blood. That is the price after many a fight.

It was his pride of course to show none of this. Feeling good, it was his happiness not to fail to offer happiness. So he paused at the door to his villa as if he wanted to give the Africans waiting outside more adequate recompense for the time they had devoted, and he roared, "I can lick anybody you got. Give me your best. I will fight your best fighter."

The thin Blacks giggled. Those who understood a little English giggled immediately, and the others took it up in ripples of laughter as his words were translated.

"Don't give me nothing but your best," said Ali.

A twelve-year-old boy came out and started shadow-boxing the air five feet in front of him. "You think you got a chance, huh?" said Ali. "You're in trouble. You're in a lot of trouble." He began to spar with the twelve-year-old, who was fast and knew a little about boxing, and Ali slowly sank to his knees and cried out, "I'm the one in trouble. He's too much for me."

Everybody roared. Ali got up and said to the boy, "You whupped me today, but watch out. I'm going to go home and practice, and then I'll come back and whip you." He saluted the crowd and returned inside.

Once more it was time to leave and say good-bye and get ready to leave Africa. Norman made his farewells to Ali and Belinda, and had a last look of Ali stretched out on the green velveteen Borox sofa, his bare feet up on the coffee table, while Belinda sitting across from him was now in her turn giggling and tickling the bare soles of his famous flying feet with a small ivory back scratcher. Farewell to Ali.

Driving on the road back to the hotel for the last time, Norman kept passing groups of young boys jogging on the shoulder. He did not know if it was a brand-new phenomenon, but squad after squad of young adolescents were out there on the dark roads, and once he almost hit a few they came up so suddenly in the lights. On the night he jogged with Ali — was it five nights ago? — Ali said afterward, "It'll be a great experience for you remembering that you ran with the Champion just a few days before the fight," and he thought it a peculiarly heavy remark at the time, but had the recognition now that it was just possible Ali was going to be right once more — already Norman was beginning to think of it fondly.

18. BAGARRE À DAKAR

THERE WAS TROUBLE getting home. It would come at Dakar, where a mob, convinced Muhammad Ali was on board, would tear over the runways of the airport and surround the plane. There was, however, no sense of this on departure from Kinshasa. Rather there was relief. Rumors had been passing that Ali and his camp would commandeer the flight. It was nice to find out at the airline desk that one's First Class seat was still intact. No small boon. To be trapped in the middle of three seats in Economy on the nineteen-hour flight from Kinshasa to New York with stops at Lagos, Accra, Monrovia and Dakar had to be one of the intimate clues life offered of suffering after death. It was one of the longest flights left in the world, and sometimes one of the worst. Still, Norman liked it. A share of the action of Africa, legal and illegal, seemed to get on and off the plane: hunters and smugglers, engineers and tribal chiefs, Black babies, and a mysterious white man in a black suit, white shirt, black tie who traveled First Class with a black leather satchel in the empty seat next to him. The seat had been purchased for the satchel and it was the only empty seat in the compartment. Who in First Class could take his eyes off the black bag? It would later develop the owner was a King's Messenger, and when a British official met him to give escort off the plane, the man in the black suit exclaimed in a fine high-service English voice, "Thank God, you're here on time." Were the contents fissionable material or secrets of state? Were they crooks in costume and the real crop prove to be diamonds? It was the only flight Norman knew which on any routine night could offer the visual impact of a Hitchcock film.

Besides, there was time to think. Hours to think and hours to read. The boredom of a long flight could turn inside out again, and boredom give way to epiphany. He had a few on the trip back. Events of the week enlarged the space he had prepared for them in his brain, but Norman's thoughts were too general and he was full of champagne, misery, pleasurable recollections and lack of sleep. He slept. His dreams he did not remember. When he awoke, it was to the my-plane-is-sure-my-turf Southern tone of the pilot saying through the public address system that he wished to assure his Pan-American passengers there would not be any trouble at Dakar, but just in case, " 'cause folks, I don't know where they got the idea, it was just a rumor at Kinshasa, but the good people of Dakar are convinced that the Heavyweight Champion is on the plane, and they want to see Muhammad Ali in person so a couple of thousand of them are out at the airport now. It's one in the morning in Dakar but out there on the runway they are sure he's here on board. We're going to come in on one of the back runways and then maybe we can discharge our outgoing and take on our incoming passengers via the airport bus. In any case, we're sorry for the delay."

But when they landed in that far-off secret place at the end of the airport, the secret had been discovered. Even as they taxied, there was the sight of hundreds of people running toward them. The pilot cut his lights, gunned his motors and the plane trundled across the airport to another runway. Other people came running toward them. The pilot cut the motors. "Folks," he said, "we've been instructed to sit tight for a while. If we keep taxiing, somebody out there might get hurt. So we'll just remain here for a spell. Everything will be all right."

In no time the plane was surrounded. It was the most peculiar situation. Police cars with red flashers on top and police cars with blue flashers kept driving slowly into the crowd, and patterns of revolving red and blue light flared in S-turns and spirals beneath the wings, and fire trucks drove up and hosed the crowd. And the plane got wet as well. Drops ran down the windows. Sitting on the ground, all doors closed, the cabin was getting hot. The police cars had given up. The plane stood at the end of a runway surrounded by near to a thousand people and every spotlight in the airport was beamed upon them. Now the plane could not start its motors without incinerating a part of the population of Dakar.

More people kept flowing out of the terminal building toward the plane, streaming across the endless asphalt acres of the airport. Cars with loudspeakers drove up to address them and then drove away. Now a passenger bus arrived and parked and waited. Outside, the crowd shifted with rumors. Individuals broke off and ran when police cruisers would start their motors. Sometimes, like an elephant thrashing in its sleep, the crowd would shift a few feet in one direction or another, as if one of the rumors had moved through their legs.

"I think," said the pilot's voice, "we've worked out a modus vivendi. The people out there don't believe us when we tell them Muhammad Ali isn't on board. So we've agreed to let a delegation come on and search the plane. They won't incommode anybody, and it may enable us to get going. Incidentally, we're going to disembark all departing passengers and take on the new ones right after the visit of the delegation."

A cheer went up from the passengers. The stewardesses brought drinks, an emergency dispensation.

Now the delegation came through. It was a fair sampling of the crowd, officers in uniform, airport officials, workers, one woman, one cutthroat, maybe twelve Black people in the delegation. They started in Economy by looking under seats, and in the bathrooms, and by the time they reached the front were becoming unhappily convinced that maybe the Heavyweight Champion was not on board. In First Class, Bob Goodman, a public relations man for the fight, put a couple of pillows on his belly and covered them with a red blanket. "Muhammad Ali is hiding here," he whispered to the delegation, and the sight of his pink round face delighted the first two Black representatives to come up the aisle, and they made a large play of peering delicately under the blanket before they began to laugh.

After the delegation left, passengers for Dakar got off,

and new passengers for New York got on, all of them walking through an aisle of police at the bottom of the mobile stairs which went up to the door of the plane. Announcements on the negative findings of the delegation were made periodically over loudspeakers, and a part of the crowd started to leave. A considerable number remained. They had been tricked too many times over the last twenty years, and over the last two thousand years, to believe a delegation. They knew Muhammad Ali was on the plane.

A stewardess went out on the platform at the top of the mobile stairs and began to talk to the crowd in French. "We would be proud to have him here," she said through an electric bullhorn. "We would want him aboard. But he is not on board. *Je vous jure. Muhammad Ali n'est pas sur l'avion.*"

The crowd looked at her. They hardly moved. She was tall and thin with a quintessential American face, honest, good-featured, strong, a hint stingy, and she would never reveal a sense of humor too quickly to strangers. The crowd heard her out in distrust. She was a representative of the powers of vested white deceit. Catcalls came to her, but not too many. Black ears hung on the revelation of American character to be heard in the vowels and consonants of her French. Besides, she was the only actor left.

Norman had gone out to get some air on the platform at the top of the stairs. Since it was even hotter outside than in the cabin and smelled of old oil and jet exhaust, he stayed only to listen to the girl. She looked at him and shrugged. "It doesn't seem to work," she said, looking down on the waiting faces below.

"May I make a suggestion?"

"I wish you would."

"Say to them that whether they believe you or not, they must know that the Champion of the world, Muhammad Ali, would never hide from his own people in a bathroom."

"That's good," said the stewardess. "That might work. How do you say bathroom?"

"Try *lavabo*."

"*Lavabo. Lavabo.*" She picked up the bullhorn and delivered his thought, working gallantly at her French. He listened for a while. "*Muhammad Ali ne veut pas cacher dans la lavabo,*" said the girl. "*Il est trop grande pour cela. Un homme trop large pour avoir peur. La champion du monde qui avait le courage de battre avec George Foreman ne cache pas dans un lavabo quand il y a opportunité pour dire bonjour à son peuple. Il vous aime. Vous êtes son peuple.*"

No, nothing much seemed to be going on. There was an air of dead disappointment in the crowd. The evening had promised much and now they were damp from their own sweat and the fire truck's hosing. After a while, Norman went back into the plane.

Some few minutes later he saw that the crowd was, indeed, beginning to disperse. In another quarter of an hour, the stewardess came in and the stairs were removed, the airplane hatch was shut, the motors started up. Cheerfully, the captain shouted through the PA to the stewardesses, "Down girls, we're about to roll."

They taxied and took off. Back in the air again, the stewardess who had been at the bullhorn came by and told him that she thought his idea had helped. He was sufficiently pleased to ask her name and explain that he was a writer and might wish to put this episode in his piece. She replied, "I think I've got to ask the captain for permission." In a little while, she returned and said, "He says it's all right to tell you. My name is Gail Toes. Mrs. Richard Toes from Schenectady, based in New York. Toes like feet," she added with a slight stiffening of her diaphragm as if her husband might never know how much a girl loved him to take the name. One of the other stewardesses passing by now stopped and said to her, "Gail, I was proud of you. Your French is getting real good."

"Well, you got to work at something," said Gail Toes. She had much time on layovers in parts of Africa she knew little about, she explained, so she studied French.

A little later on the high trip over the Atlantic with the lights out and most of the passengers asleep, Norman played a game with the stewardesses in their forward compartment. It was something with five dice and many ways of counting bonuses, and he was not very good at it and lost by thousands of points, much to their amusement. Finally he went to sleep and had a few hours before they put down in New York, and did not remember the game until some weeks later when, thinking of it, he sent each of the girls an autographed copy of the softcover edition of *Marilyn* and expressed the hope they would think his ability to write was somewhat greater than his flair for dice.

19. LUCKY, THE THREE-TIME LOSER

WOULD YOU LIKE more of an ending? Here is an African tale. A tribal chief lent a sheep to a friend of Father Tempels. One morning the sheep was found dead. A dog belonging to the friend was found eating it. There was no evidence the dog had killed the sheep, indeed it probably died in its sleep. Still, the friend, whose name was Kapundwe, happened to be a chief himself, and he made reparations to the first chief. The animal, after all, had been in his care. So he gave back not one sheep but three and added a hundred francs. This large repayment was to compensate the first chief properly for his feeling that he had suffered something more than the mere loss of an animal. The shocking disappearance of his possession had disturbed his vital force. "His peaceful enjoyment of life" had been "wounded." The payment, therefore, was to recognize his natural rights to a "restoration of being." Both chiefs understood the transaction perfectly.

We are speaking of the economy of mood. Maybe it is the only economy in the play of forces between those who are living and those who are dead. Of course, we will hardly know until an African becomes emperor of the moon.

About the Author

Born in 1923 in Long Branch, New Jersey, and raised in Brooklyn, NORMAN MAILER was one of the most influential writers of the second half of the twentieth century and a leading public intellectual for nearly sixty years. He is the author of more than forty books. *The Castle in the Forest,* his last novel, was his eleventh *New York Times* bestseller. His first novel, *The Naked and the Dead,* has never gone out of print. His 1968 nonfiction narrative, *The Armies of the Night,* won the Pulitzer Prize and the National Book Award. He won a second Pulitzer for *The Executioner's Song* and is the only person to date to have won Pulitzers in both fiction and nonfiction. Five of his books were nominated for National Book Awards, and he won a lifetime achievement award from the National Book Foundation in 2005. Mr. Mailer died in 2007 in New York City.